Fabrics.....Reconstructed

a collection of surface changes

by Lois Ericson

Photographs: Jim Fyfe
Unless otherwise noted.

Guest Artist:
Ardyth Davis
Leesburg, Va.

Very Special Thanks To
My Friends:

Hedi....the seamstress
Bets....the enthusiast
Mary........the typist
Lennart.....the editor

ISBN 0-911985-03-4

To Linda, Diane, Kristine and Michael
who have, each in their own special
way, shared my life and contributed
immensely to my growth.

Contents

"In art, it is nothing to follow
it is everything to discover."

From a lecture by Magdalena Abakanowicz
Convergence '84, Dallas

At this particular time in my life, discovery seems to be the key word. I love to experiment! This book is a sharing of those experiments and concepts with you. There is no suggestion of a project or object to make, simply ideas to expand upon....a starting point to hopefully inspire or motivate.

Changing the surfaces of fabrics/fibers has always been fascinating to me...both as a weaver and as a clothing designer. I enjoy choosing a flat, sometimes uninteresting piece of material and recontructing it...seeing it change and become something new and exciting. When I discover a new or different way to solve a problem...for me, that's JOY!

If this book serves only to give you the courage to bend or break a rule or two, to take you one step further...then this has been an endeavor worthwhile. ENJOY!

General Information

Start by being observant, really looking at the textures in your everyday world. Jot down ideas, either real or imagined possibilities. Sometimes we just get a glimpse of something... the view from a plane or from a passing car...the things that we think we see can be more interesting than if we had time to study them carefully. When you record your impressions, it is helpful to write the terms that will remind you of the textures that will be translated to a fabric technique (e.g., looked like woven strips or big, stuffed tucks).

A sketchpad or notebook is a must to record your observations. You will soon see that your sketchpad full of ideas and notes will be invaluable. You will have an unlimited supply from which to draw.

I'd like to say a few words about creativity. Good news! Everybody has it! The more you use it, the more 'finely tuned' it becomes. There is a never ending supply of ideas... they usually come faster than one can act on them.

The next logical step is to simulate, in fabric, a texture you've seen and recorded in your notebook.

Review the techniques you already know...there are probably many in your repertoire that will be adaptable to the texture you are about to construct.

The examples in this book are a very small sampling of the possibilities. I'm sure that you will be able to add many new ones to this collection. I encourage you to experiment and have fun. Try ideas and combinations that maybe you have never seen put together. Stretching a familiar technique to its limits...may be the answer to your texture 'question'. When we always do something the same way, we don't learn anything new...we have to reach beyond our normal routine. Remember, the only limits we have are those we place on ourselves.

Stitching

Surface interest can begin with very simply concepts. Stitching is probably the easiest of all the techniques and can be an effective method to use when very little change is desired.

I have used buttonhole twist on this example, as it is one way to make the stitching appear a little bolder. The lines were stitched; then the thread ends, left long, were threaded through a sewing needle. French knots were sewn at the ends. Another possibility would be to use two sewing threads through the needle in your machine.

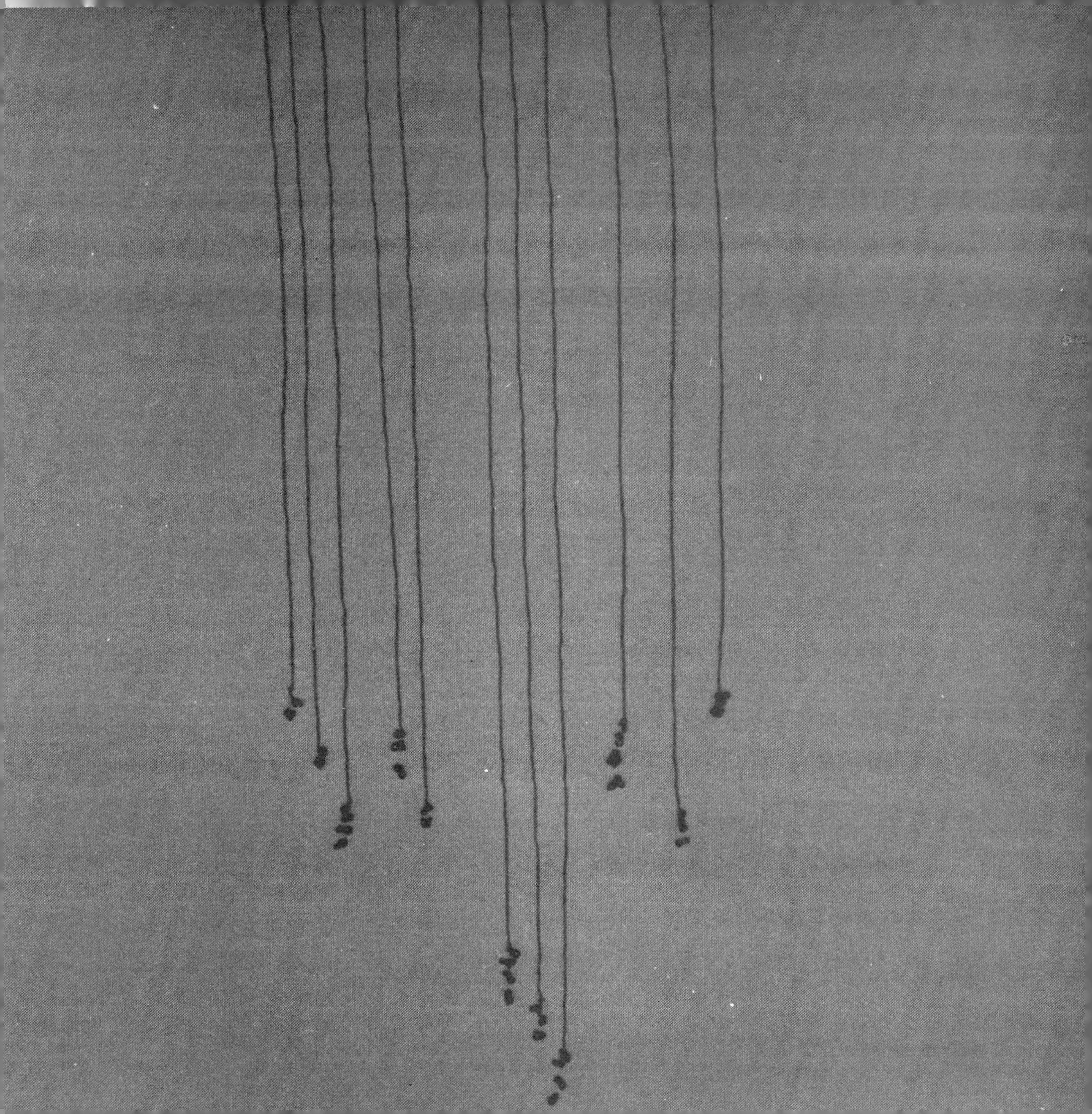

If guidelines are needed for your stitching, there are various marking pens available. (Some lines disappear after a time period, some marks are removed with water.) The stitching, at the ends, that looks like wheat, is easy if you use your sewing machine reverse lever, flipping it back and forth.

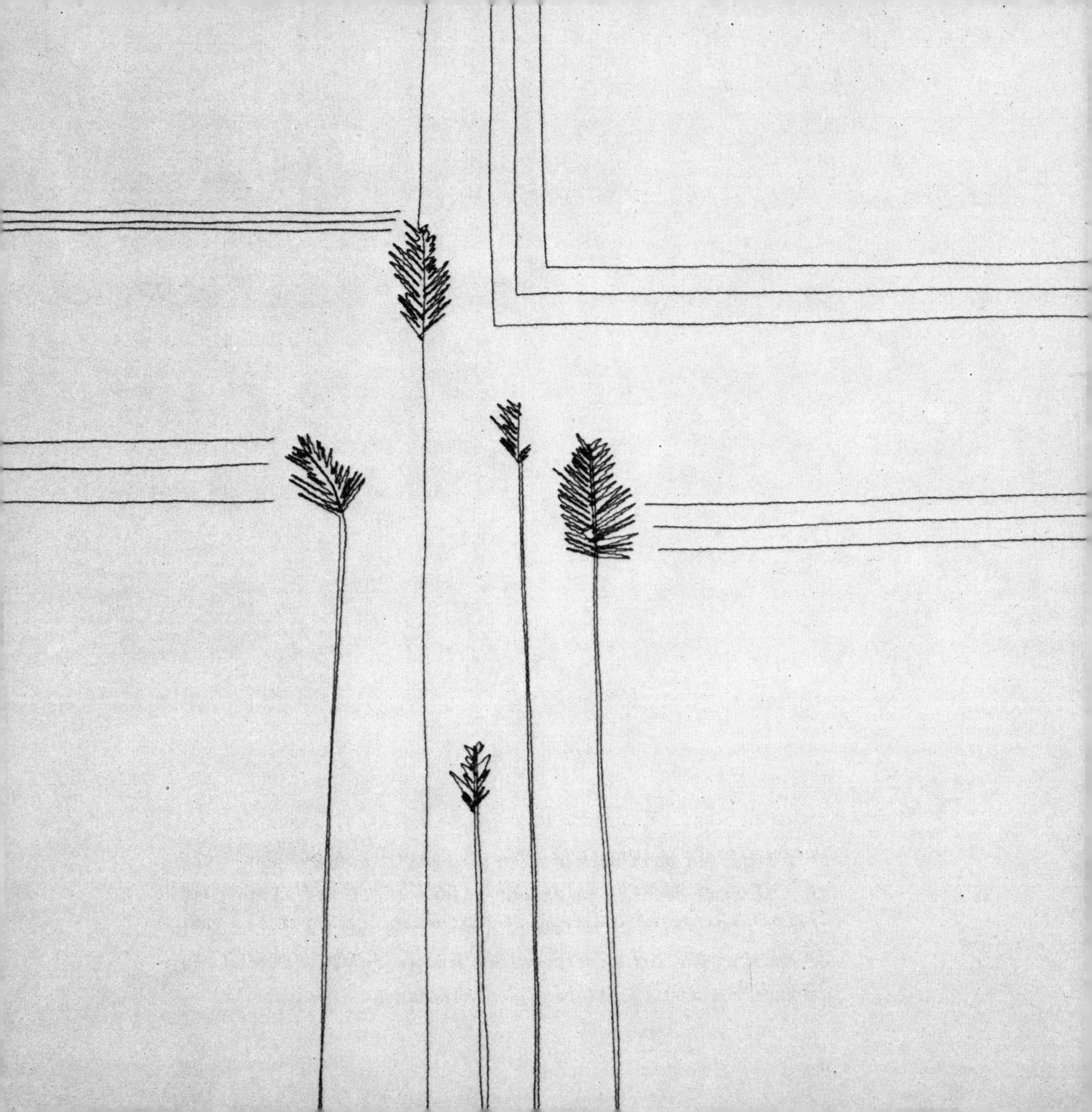

Draw lines on your fabric with a sewer's marking pen. Stitch with single, double, or triple needle (if there is an oval throat plate on your machine, a multiple needle can usually be used.) The patterns possible are infinite...that's why we have our trusty notebook for reference.

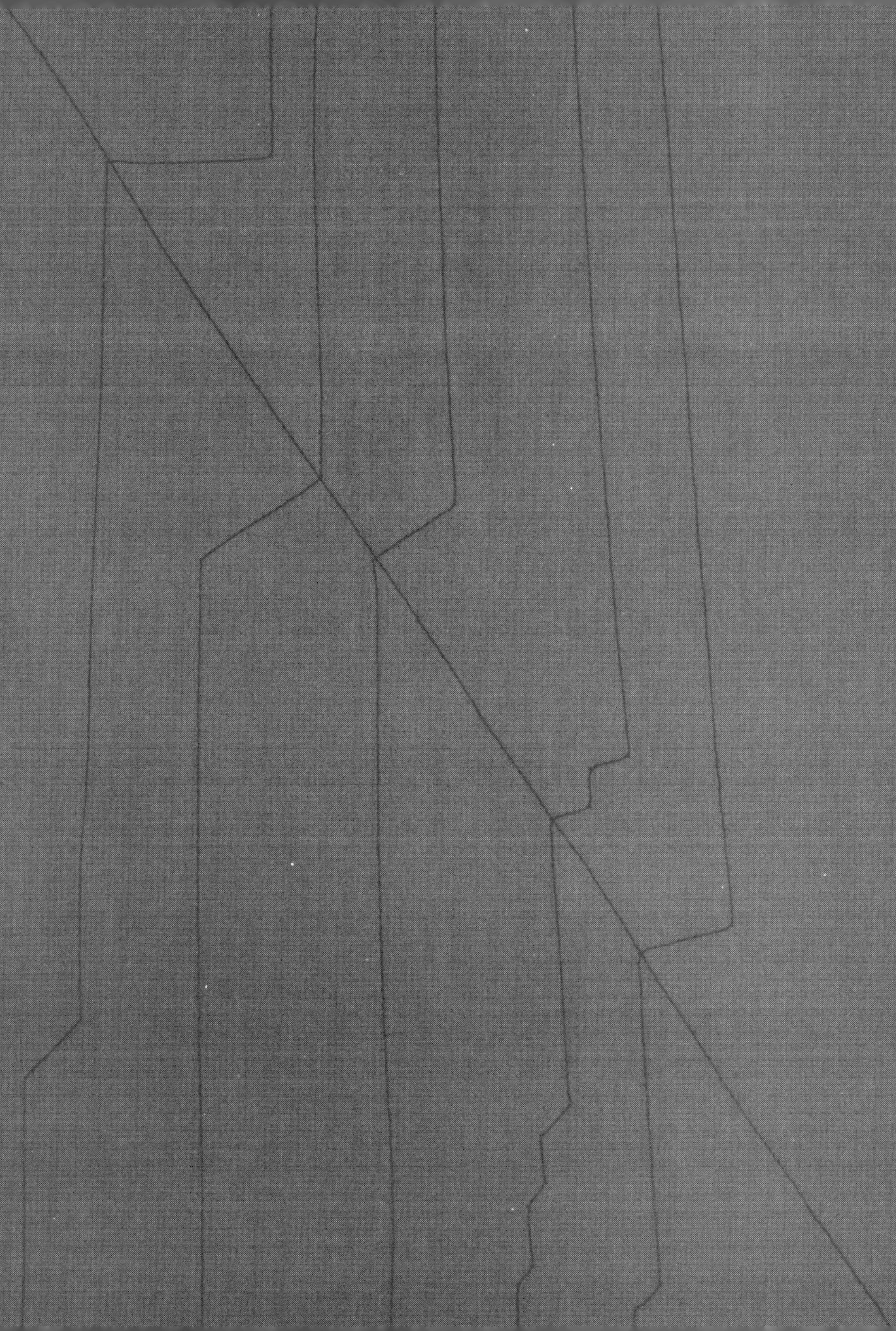

This pattern was noted from a plane somewhere above the Mid-west...the sections came together. The lines were similar but not the same in each square.

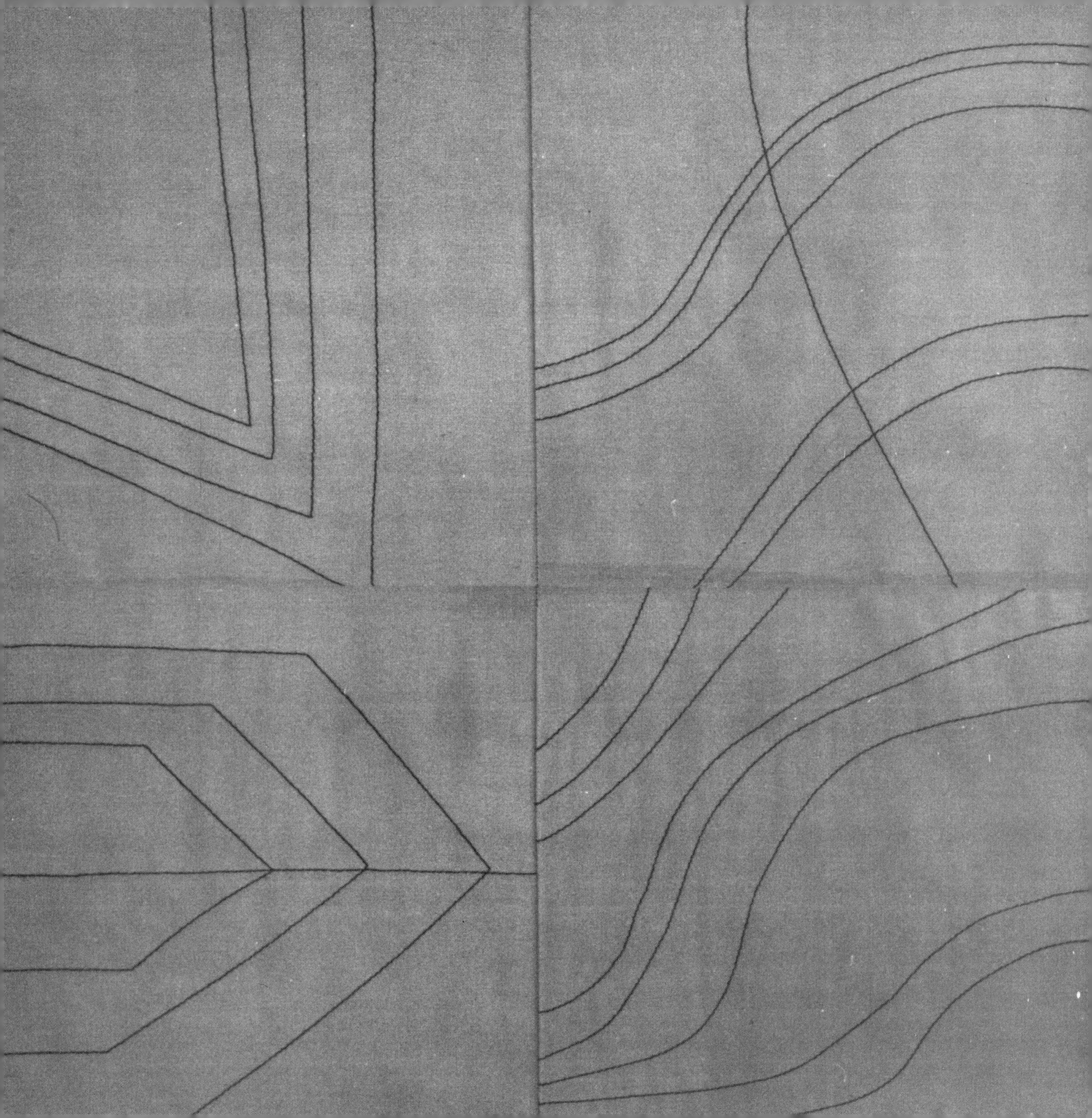

An object, even an insignificant one, can be emphasized and made more important by repeated stitching lines around the object.

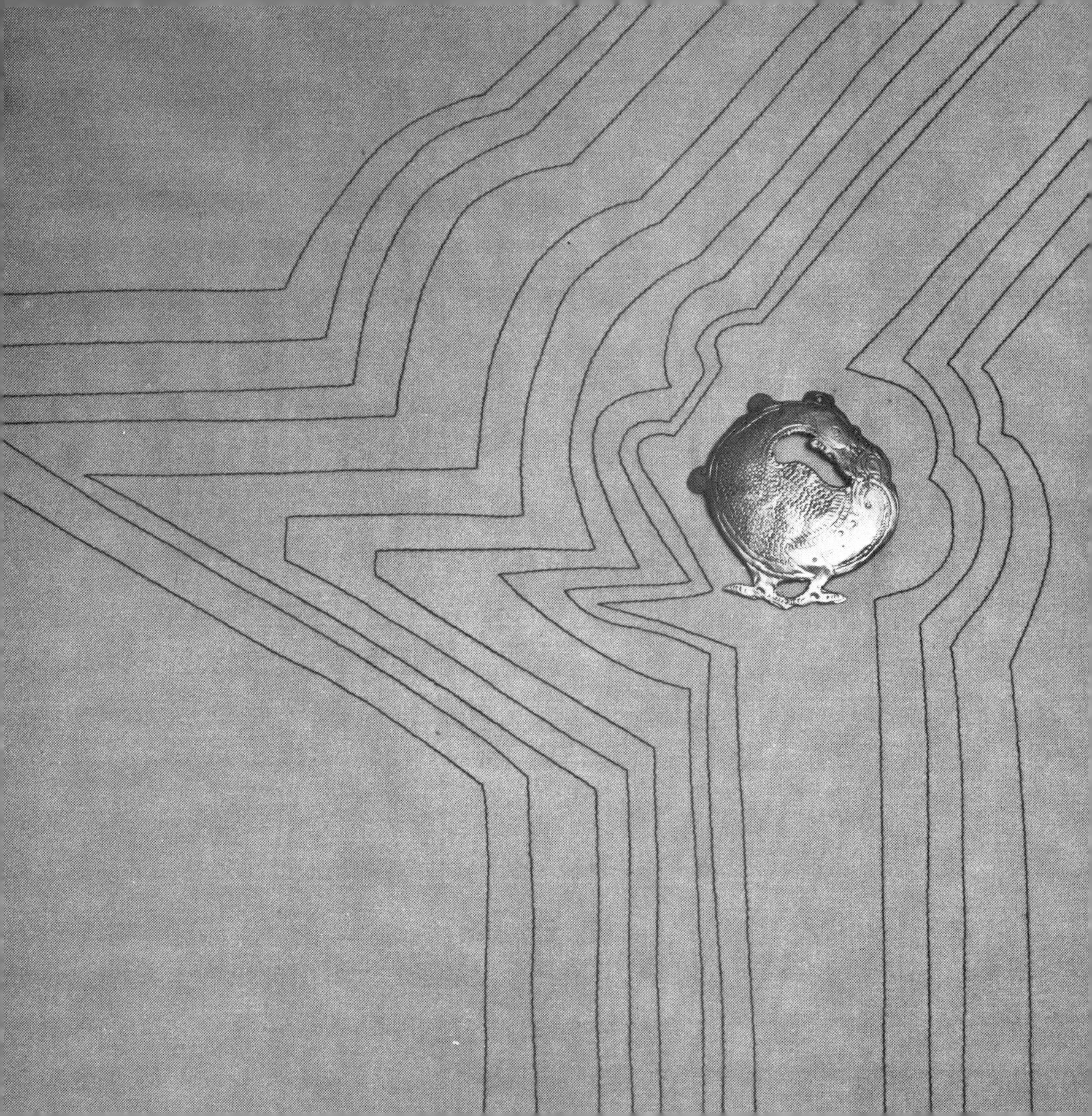

A metallic or bouclé thread (even thin, narrow ribbon) can be wound on your bobbin, when that thread cannot be successfully threaded through the needle. You may have to hand wind it on, the result is well worth the effort. Simply stitch on the wrong side of your fabric. Draw guidelines, if needed, with your 'sewing pen'.

Cutting up one piece of fabric and putting it back together will be more interesting if you stitch on the pieces after they are cut up and before they are reassembled. This can also be effective if several shades of one color fabric are used together.

Couching refers to a method of attaching threads or groups of threads to a background. Most often this stitching technique is done by hand. However, I found that using the small width zig-zag stitch on my machine worked perfectly. I used some thick and thin cotton string for this sample. For a softer effect I placed thin batting under the fabric... then stitched through all layers and string.

The very simple piecing is made more dramatic by adding some chenille yarn. It is amazing that this zig-zag stitching doesn't show, even close up. Of course, the thread should match.

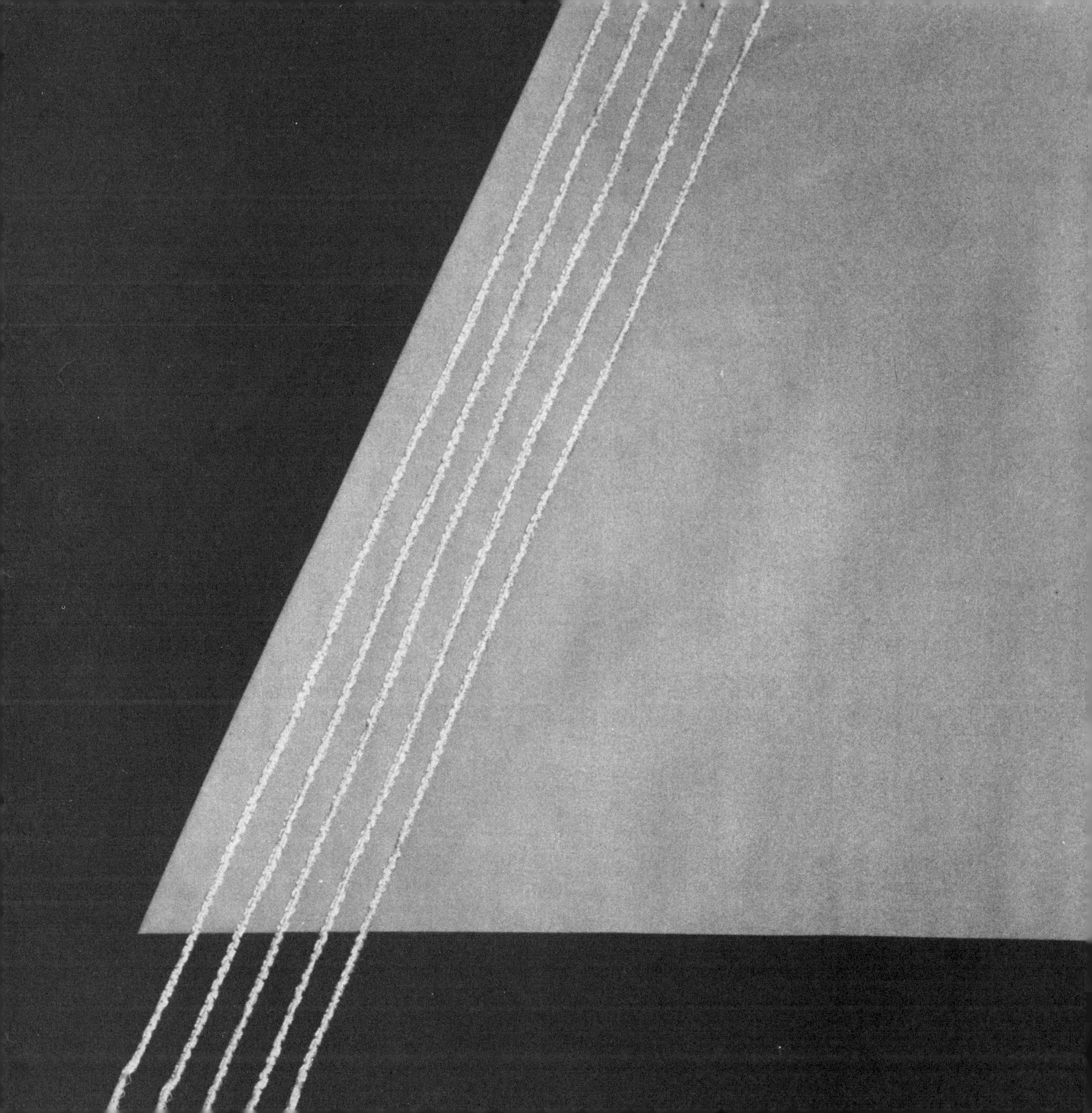

This design was inspired by an aerial photograph of a train yard, in the book The World From Above. This is one example of the double-needle stitching. Long straight or curvy lines are easiest to do. Turning sharp corners is a challenge, as you will see when you try it. Using two shades of a color or two entirely different colors of thread gives a whole new dimension to your stitching.

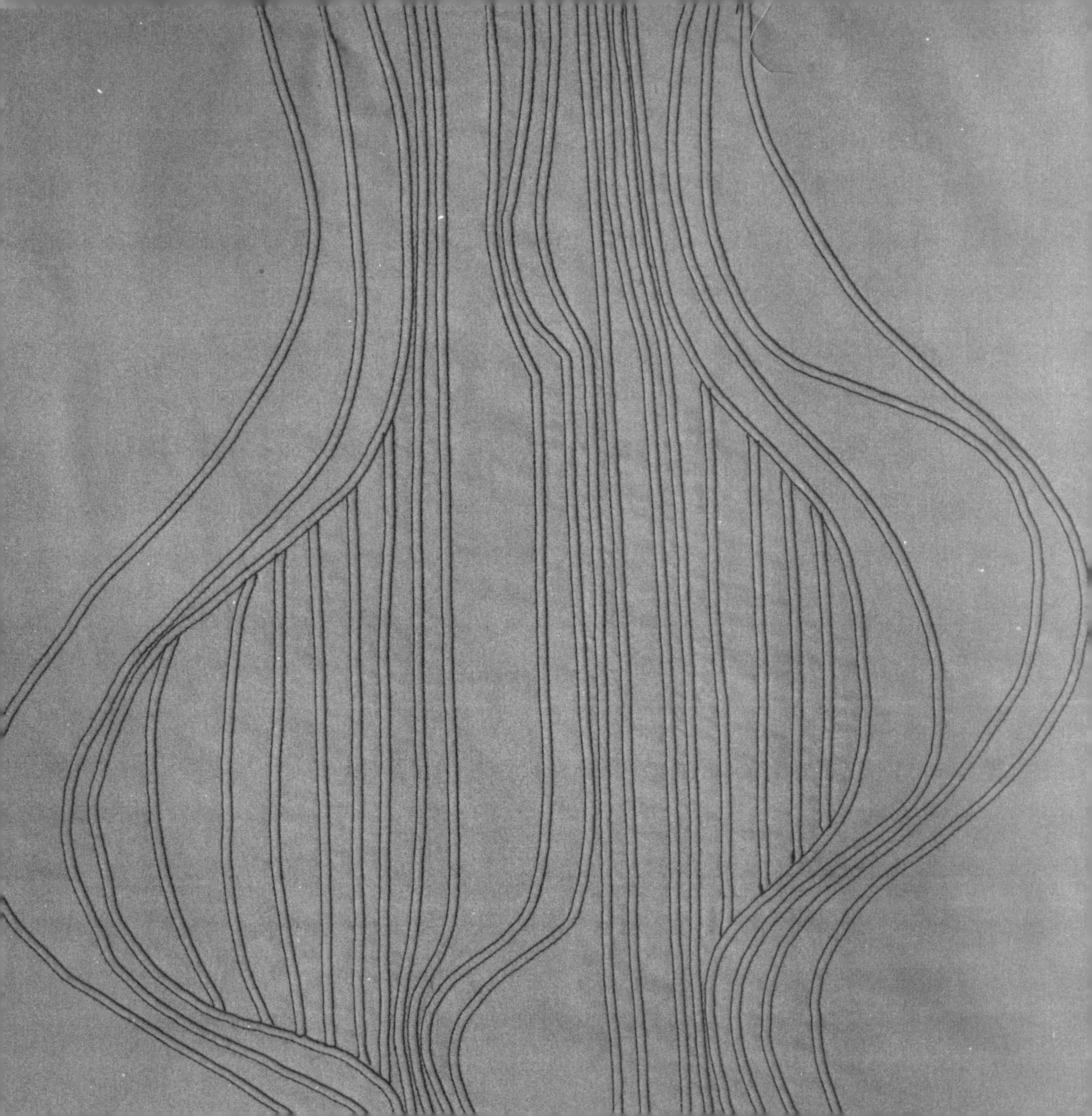

Decorative stitching is combined with leather and some faced shapes. Applying pieces that have facings to finish the edges make it so easy...this leads us into the next section on faced shapes.

Faced Shapes

The word applique always brings to mind this image of tedious hand stitching of edges that never wanted to stay turned under. To simplify that process for myself, I cut facings or bias strips for the edges to be finished, in the same or contrasting material. If a bias strip is used, the edges of the entire shape can be finished, if desired. Simply stitch the 1½" (or wider) bias strip to the edge to be finished. Turn and press.

If a facing, the size of the whole shape, is used to finish the edge...one, two or three sides will be left open, depending on your design. This opening will be used to turn the faced piece to the right side after trimming. So stitch, trim, turn and press. These shapes can then be applied easily by machine stitching or tacking by hand.

Use a marking pen to draw guidelines on your underlining (old sheets are great, not <u>too</u> old, of course). I usually cut the pieces that relate to my drawing and place them on my underlining...on this particular one I started in the center and worked to the outside. After the first few decisions have been made...I sew the facings on, trim and turn, press my pieces. I pin the pieces in place on the underlining, arranging and changing as I proceed.

Various textures are combined in this piece. With few colors, the textures are accentuated and automatically command your attention.

Photographs in many kinds of books can be inspiring. The arches on this page were translated to fabric from a book on architectural details. Each shape was cut, faced and overlapped. Each layer was stitched in place, starting with the smaller, lower one.

Windows and doors in an arranged pattern can be a starting point for faced 'holes' or shapes. Where the shapes are to be emphasized, consider using a high contrast of color for the facings. The narrow line that shows around the shapes looks like a thin piping. This line can show more or less depending on how it is pressed.

Repeating one shape can lend unity to a piece. On this example, the lower section can be the outer shape...especially interesting on the lower edge of a garment...what a relief to see an alternative to a straight around hem!

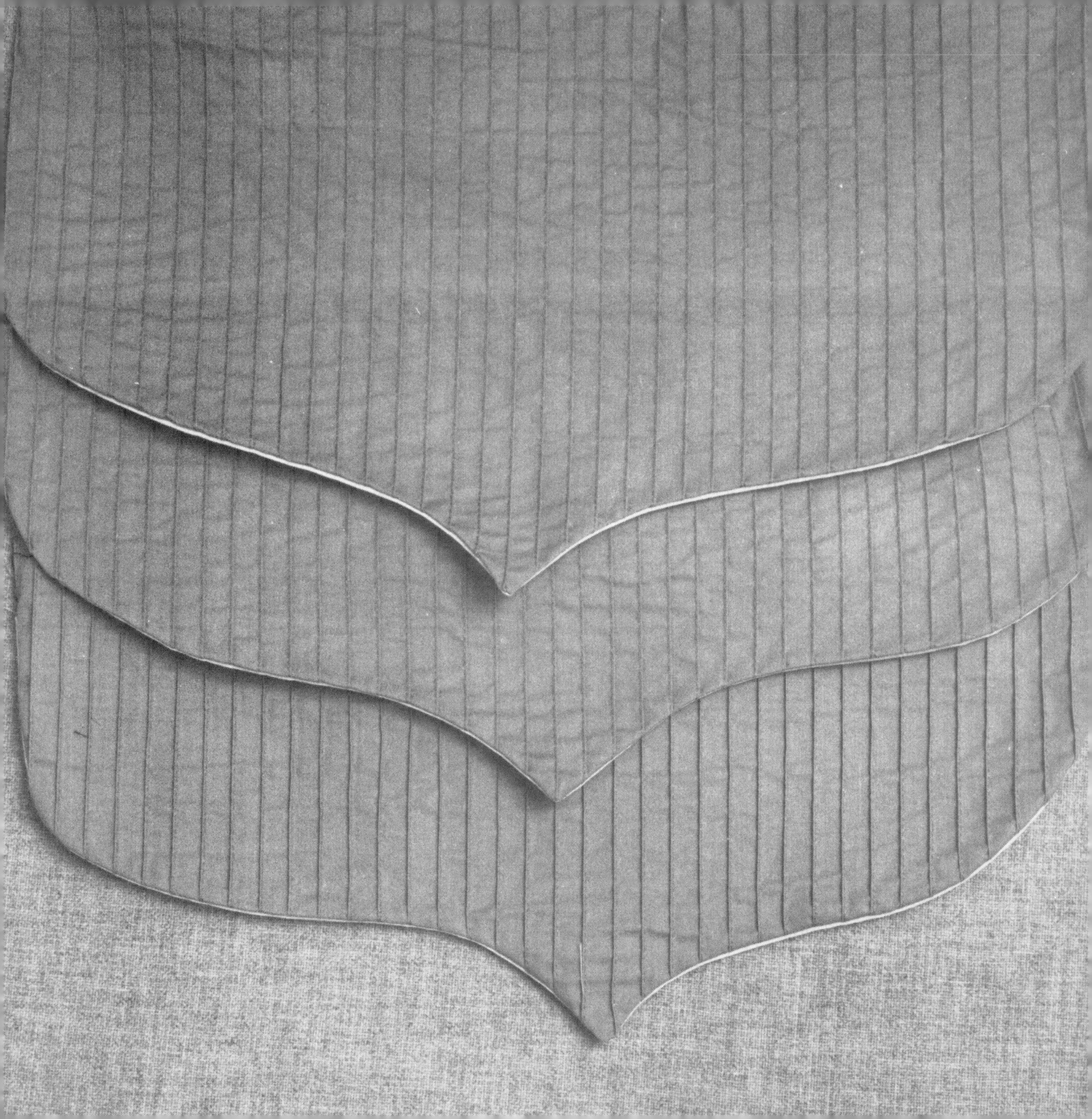

This example shows the realignment of stripes and the break-up of space. The edges of the striped fabric were cut up into a shape. The facing was stitched on... turned and pressed. This faced shape was stitched to the background fabric, then cut into strips. The strips were sewn, in order, to an underlining material.

The rounded shapes in the center are finished with bias strips. The top part is finished with pieced strips. The lower section is tubes that are loose and uneven at the ends. This directs us to the next section on tubes and strips.

Tubes & Strips

Tubes can be any width, in fact a variety is certainly more interesting and has more vitality.

Cut the strips whatever width you choose...usually mine are 1" to 3". Fold the strips in half lengthwise, right sides together, and stitch the edges. Turn and press. It is easier to turn if you stitch one end closed and turn with a chop stick, metal rod or knitting needle.

If the back of the tube isn't going to show, fold with wrong sides together and stitch along the long side and press with the seam in the middle of the back...don't turn. (No one will see the cut edges!)

Pin the tubes at an angle, at one end to the background fabric. These warps can be close together or separated, as desired. The tubes woven in the opposite direction are called the wefts. These wefts will be threaded over and under across the warps. Stitch across the ends of the strips when all are woven.

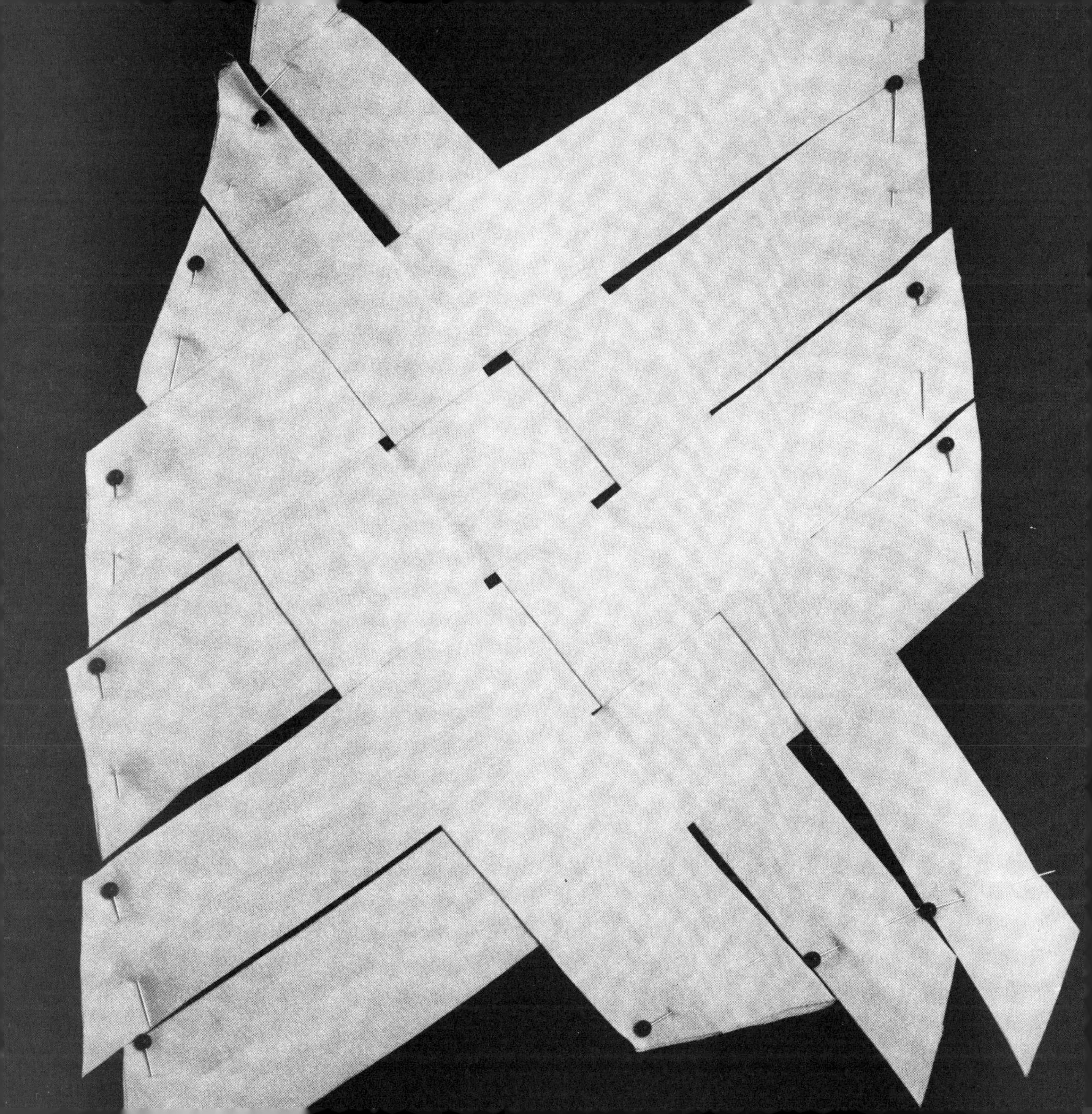

In this example, there are two distinctly different sizes of tubes. Random knotting of the narrow tubes gives this sample some needed pizazz.

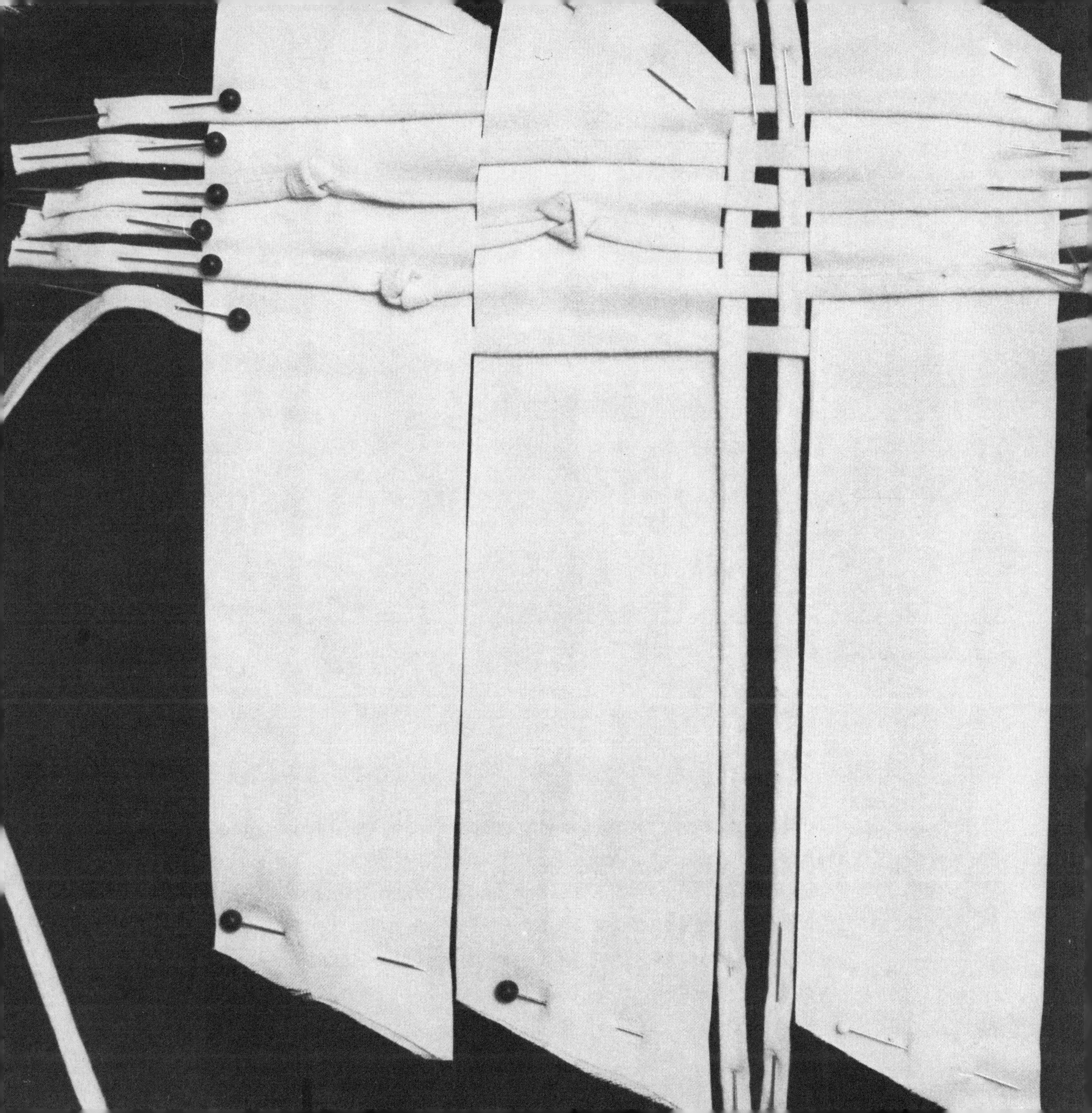

Combining woven strips with some strips that have faced shapes on the ends could be a starting point. So many possibilities for the shaped ends...they can overlap or be alternated with straight strips that may be the length of the piece. In that case, the shaped ones would be less prominent.

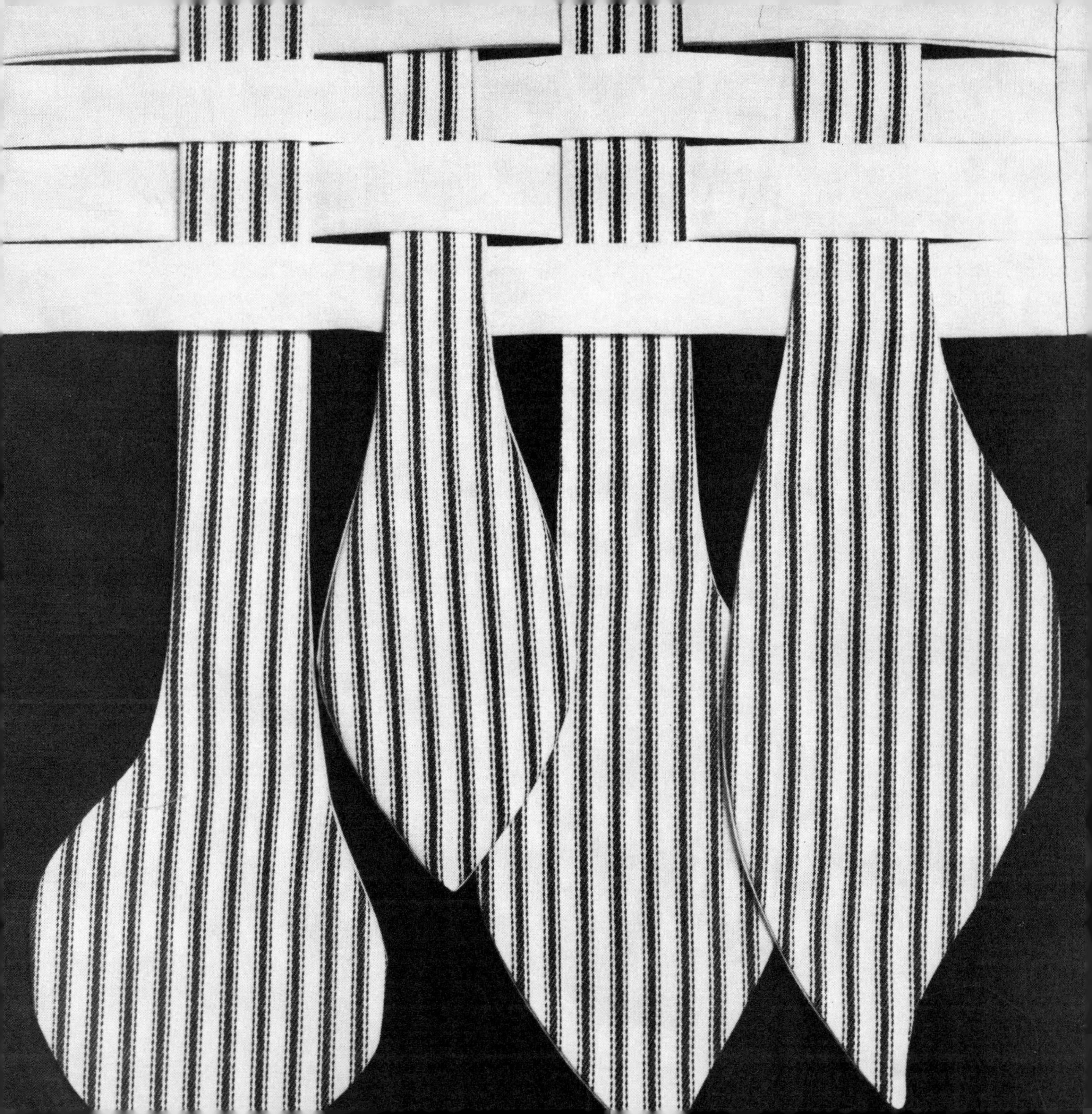

On this piece, the tubes are placed side by side and stitched to a background fabric. Notice the uneven 'hem'. If the tubes are to be the reconstructed 'fabric' without being fastened to another fabric, pin the tubes onto a sheet of tissue paper. Stitch through the tubes and paper, tear away the tissue.

Woven tubes of striped fabric that are cut lengthwise, crosswise and on the bias make this example an eye-catching one. The ends of the strips are finished with a piece of fabric in a matching plain color. A few of the strips are also plain...note the shape of the piece in the middle of this woven sample.

Try using strips of fabric as posts to divide the spaces on a printed fabric to change the image.

Woven tubes are combined with a faced shape that is stuffed.

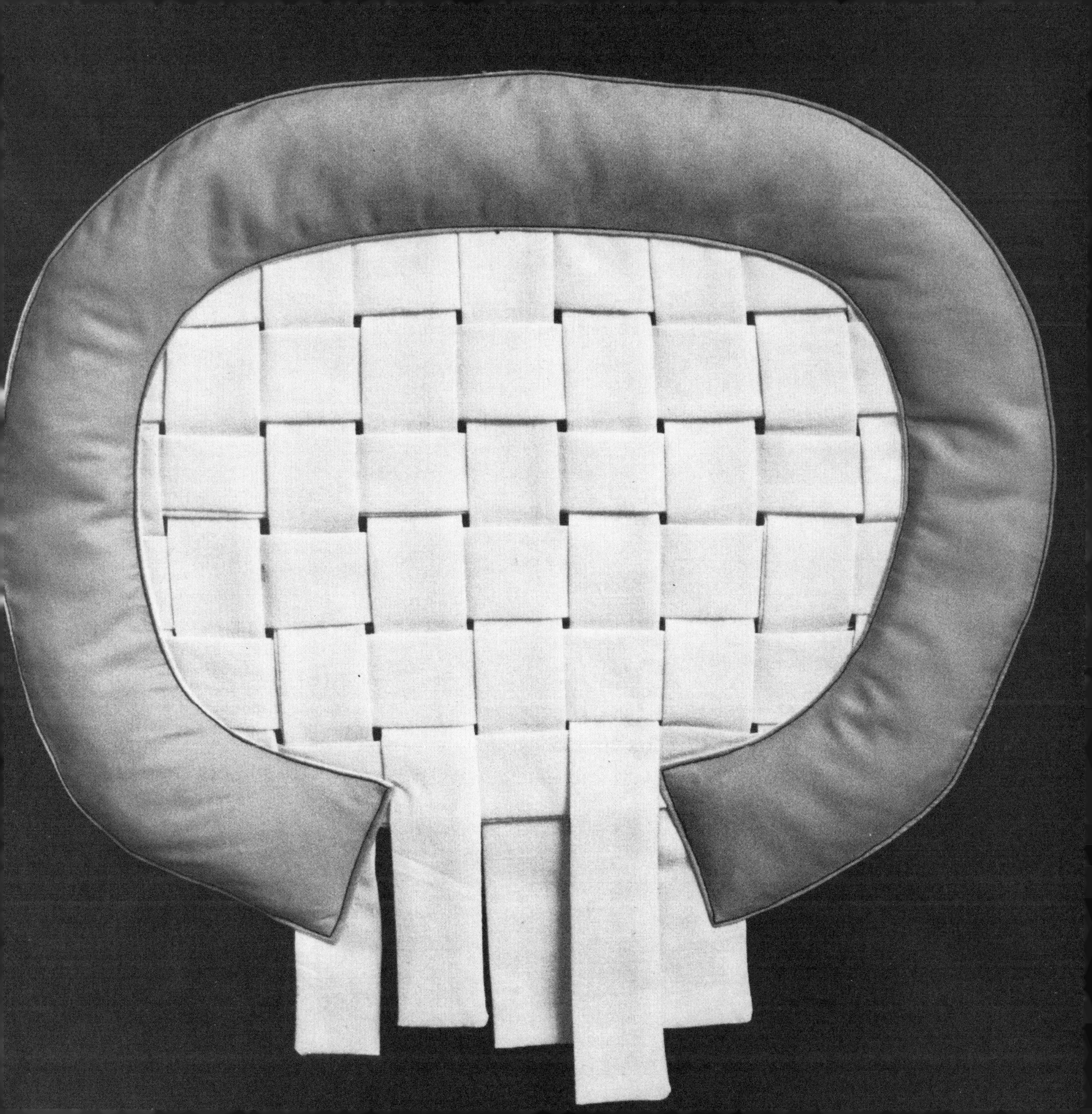

Cut the strips of fabric at least 1" wider than necessary to accommodate the welting and 1/2 to 1/3 longer than the length of the welting, to gather it. Welting can be found at most fabric or upholstery stores, and comes in many sizes.

Stitch the strips into tubes and turn them if necessary (if the seams don't show, no need to turn). Pull the welting through the stitched and turned tubes. It will, of course, wrinkle because it's too long...nice effect.

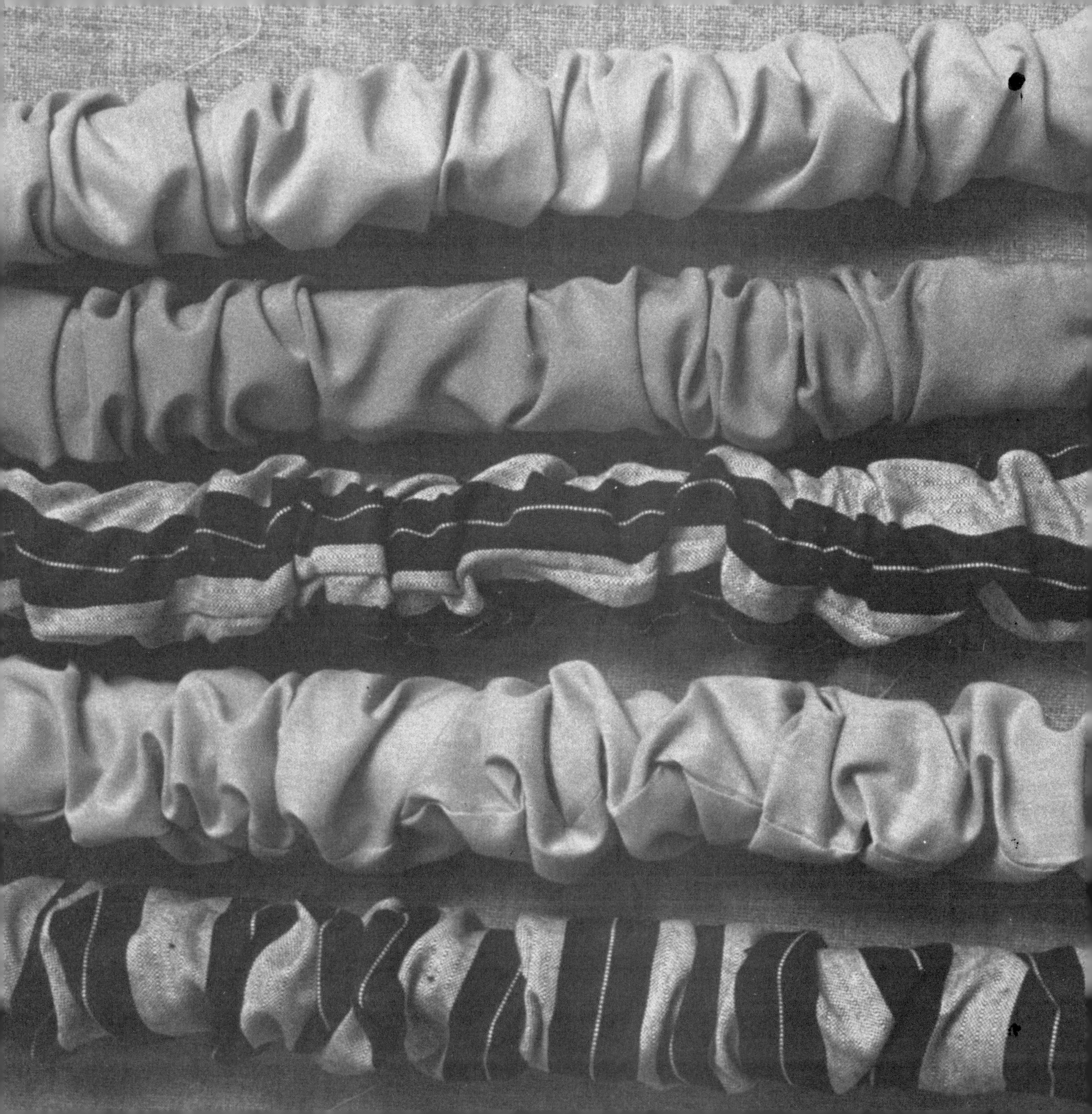

This example combines some tubes with piecing. The horizontal strips are folded over the vertical ones. The ends are covered with a strip patchwork technique. Our next section is on piecing, so let's explore it.

Piecing

Is there life after log cabin piecing???? Oh, yes!

Piecing 'by any other name' is still a method of putting sections of fabric together...might also be called patchwork or strip patchwork. The word 'piecing' seems to encompass many related techniques. The main point I'd like to make in this section is that piecing doesn't have to be monotonous and uninteresting.

The method I use is to place the first piece of fabric on the underlining. I start either at the center of my design or at one edge working to the other. Each succeeding piece of fabric covers the raw edge of the previous piece, so there is basically no handwork.

This bold graphic is a very effective sample of piecing. Each vertical strip was pieced before overlapping and sewing the strips together. The design moves from one piece to the next without exactly matching.

Starting with the triangles, place them in position first. The horizontal piece directly under that would be next. Stitch the cording to the edge of the large piece on the left and turn the edge under, press. Top-stitch in place. The horizontal bands that finish the piece are stitched by machine.

The illusion of depth is very possible with the arrangement of pieces, as in this example. Start in the center and work toward the outside...using a variety of textures or shaded colors would add considerable surface interest.

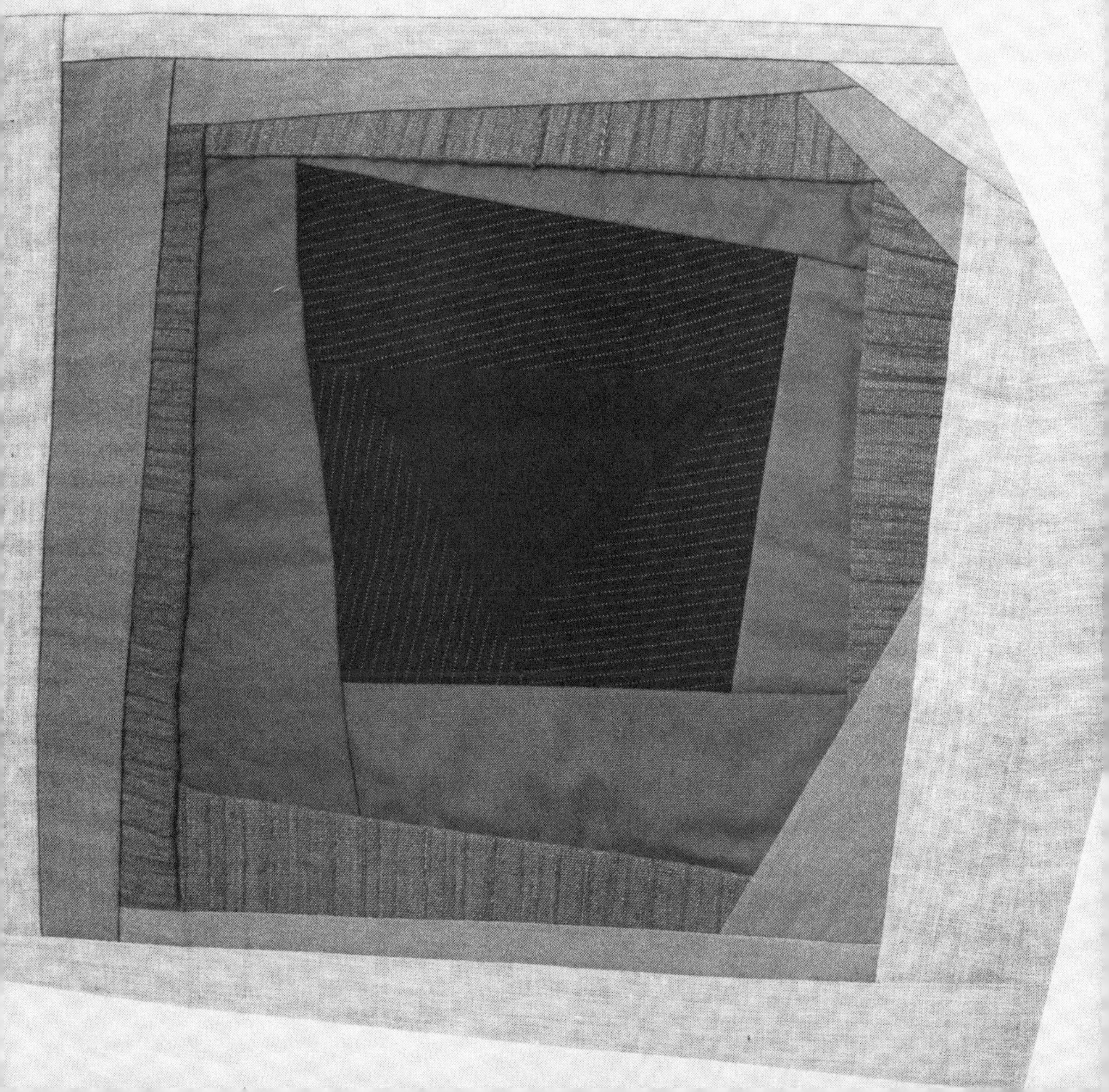

This strip patchwork was inspired by a photograph of a wooden tunnel. The bottom of each board was painted red...not evenly matched, I might add...very effective. This piece was also started in the center and worked up, across and down the other side with the strips.

The use of perspective in a pieced fabric can be very dynamic. First I drew a few guidelines on the underlining. I started piecing in the center at the doorway and worked each section toward the windows and the sunlight/shadows on the opposite wall.

The textured fabric is made up of tiny machine stitched tucks...great when you find the material already tucked... saves a lot of time. The wedge shaped inserts with the dark edges are a nice contrast to the commercially tucked material.

When piecing, there are many possibilities for inserting sections that are not strips of fabric, per se. In this patchwork, a strip of unravelled coarse cotton fabric is set in so that the fringe is a part of the design.

The little tufts of fur are stitched in as the strips of fabric are sewn. There are, of course, many other possibilities for insertion.

Cutting up a print and putting it back together with small strips of fabric, in this case striped bias... can certainly liven up an ordinary print.

This sample is also a cut up print...cutting and inserting pieces on the diagonal lend movement to this fabric from Japan.

A silk-screened iris print has been cut up. The plain sections in between are the widest and unexpectedly are the more important. Notice that the center piece, with the stems, is turned horizontally so that it doesn't line up with the other vertical stems.

A medium value material is combined with black on the inserts and the stitching for a nice contrast. The stitching takes place after each strip is sewn on. Flipping the reverse lever, back and forth, makes this 'nervous' stitching easy.

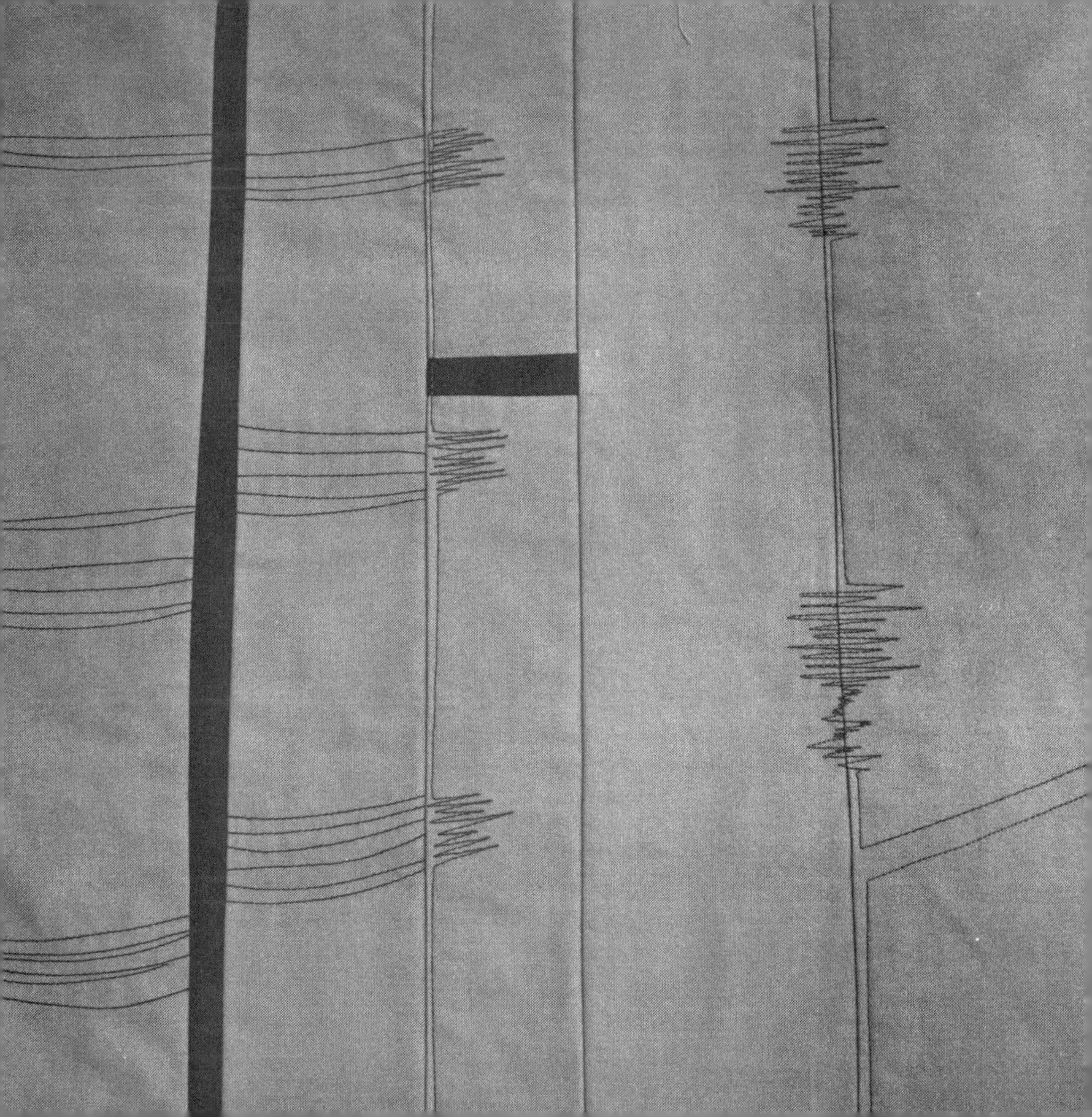

Each strip is assembled separately to combine with other strips. As they are set in place, the inserts can be adjusted to line up where desired. I normally choose a random placement, for interest. Stripes, cut in any direction, can be a great addition to the pieced strips. The stripes, then, lead us to the next section...on stripes, of course.

Stripes

I personally am very fascinated by the potential in this sometimes mundane pattern. There are also striped examples in other sections of the book, see 'nearly smocked' and 'tucks/pleats'. Stripes are so versatile and can be used effectively in most all sewing techniques.

Striped fabric that is cut into strips has great visual 'movement' and can be manipulated in an undulating way. The pieces, in this case, would be sewn together, strip patchwork fashion, to an underlining.

Piecing stripes together to make a chevron pattern is easy. It is easier if your fabric is a woven stripe so that either side is useable. Simply cut the bias strip and turn every other one to the 'wrong' side of the material.

If the stripes are printed, you will need to cut your bias strips from opposite sides, so they will come together at an angle.

This is an arrangement of stripes with random angles and lines. Start somewhere in the center and work toward the outside, making the decisions as you proceed.

Seaming sections together and leaving openings in those seams...leaves us the option of placing something underneath to show through. Additional topstitching would define those slits even more.

Striped fabric is pieced and smocked in this composite sample. The stitching lines repeat the lines and angles. A couple of the channels are stuffed (trapunto). The next section deals with contemporary smocking.

Nearly Smocked

I say nearly smocked, because I stop short of the organized and embroidered product that we normally think of as smocking. A pleater simplifies the procedure and makes it fun, instead of tedious.
Of course, you can also do the dots with the handstitching and get the same effect.

I pleat the fabric, using a double thread. I next arrange the pleats and place this fabric on an underlining. Stitch through all thicknesses on the machine to hold in place. I leave the 'gathering' threads in. Word of caution...soft, light, thin fabrics work best with the pleater...replacing many broken needles helped to draw this conclusion.

To get this undulating effect I angled the fabric right to left as the fabric is fed into the pleater. The stripes did the rest. When I get a new 'toy' such as the pleater, I experiment with it to see what new ideas materialize. I give myself permission to play...and to fail...it's all right to do both.

Try using textured fabrics with the pleating...these were crepe-like gauzes that had an interesting texture when smocked.

Very sheer fabric, such as this silk organza, was folded and creased as it was fed into the machine for pleating. The folded images and patterns were spontaneous...a nice surprise.

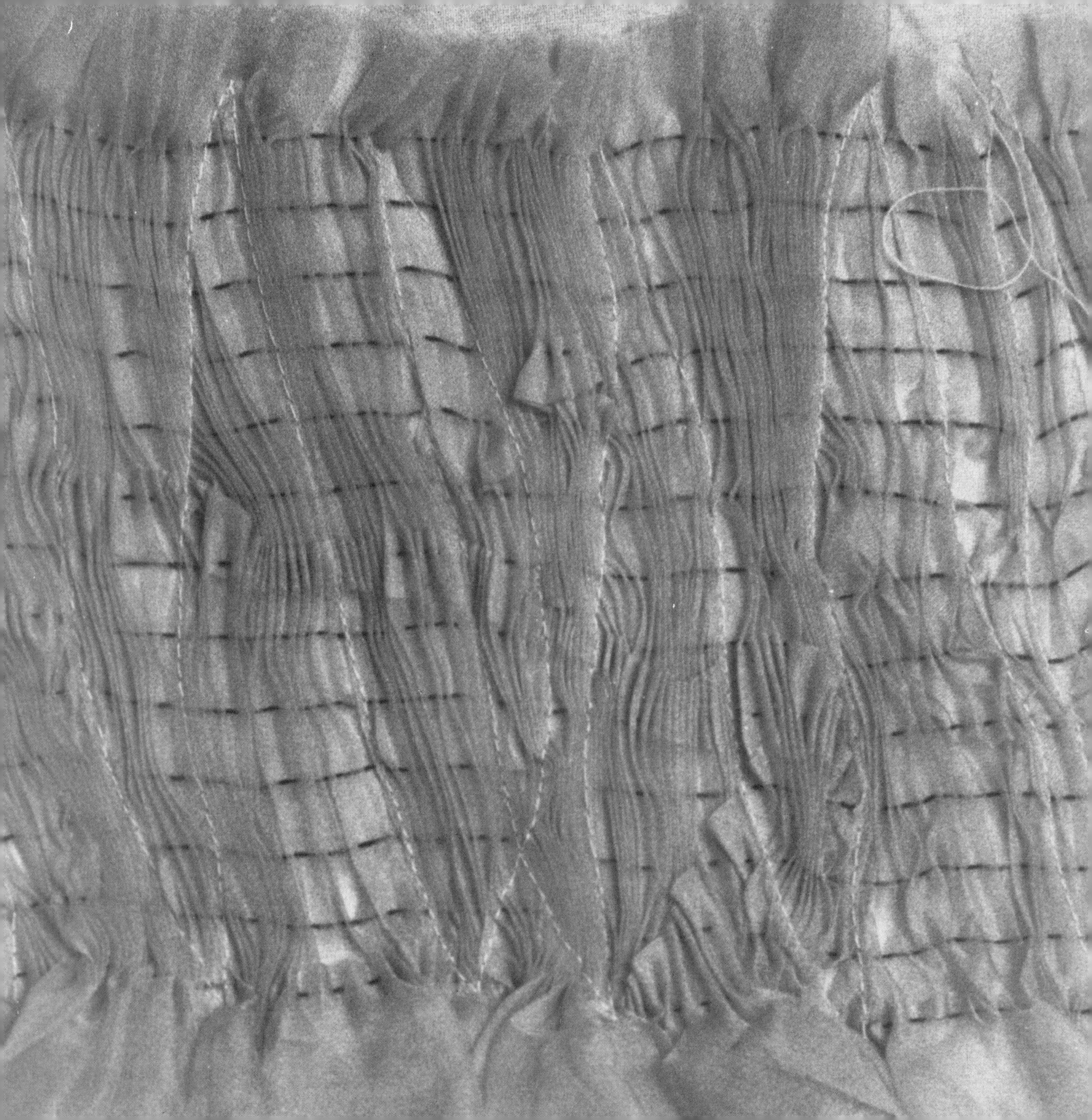

Many yards of 8" to 10" wide strips of batiste fabric were pleated and densely 'gathered'. These were stitched to an underlining and the edges of the strips were covered with a printed bias strip to finish.

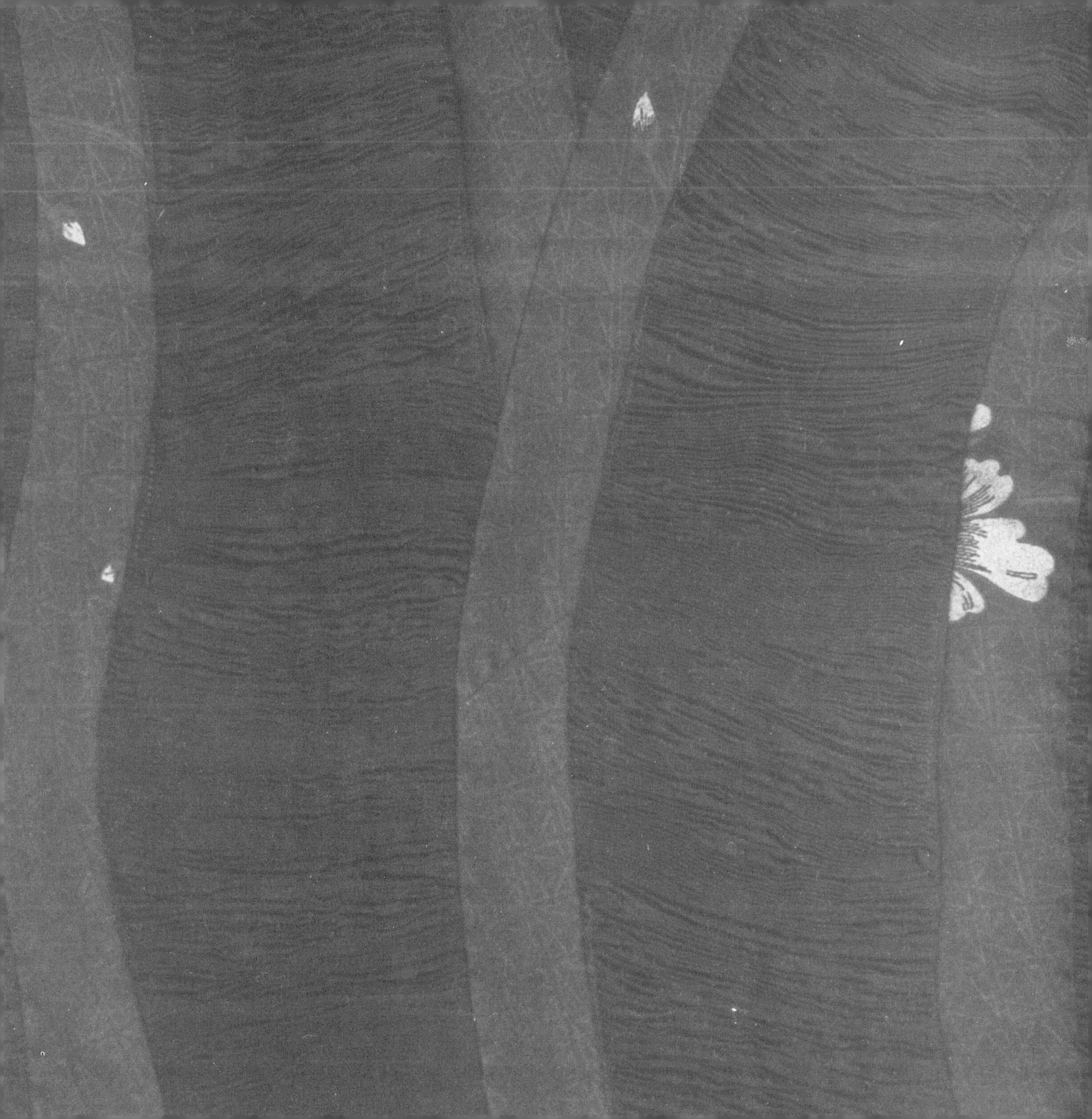

There are many possibilities for pattern and design, in the arrangement of pleated/gathered fabric. Place the prepared fabric on an underlining. Machine stitching lines will keep the gathers in place. I usually start at one side and pin, then stitch as the design takes shape.

Wrinkled/Stitched

A wrinkle is defined as a small furrow, ridge or crease on a normally smooth surface caused by crumpling, folding or shrinking. That is exactly what we are going to do in this section. Any natural fiber, or combination of natural materials, wrinkles... as we know all too well. Natural fibers are the best choice for this reconstruction project. The wrinkles fall out of man-made fabrics before they can be stitched in place.

Slightly dampen the fabric. Gather, pleat or crumple the fabric in your hands and tie to keep in place as it dries. When dry, untie and place fabric on an underlining. On occasion I have just piled the fabric on the ironing board and ironed the wrinkles in. Starting at one side, pin and arrange the wrinkles, as desired. Stitch as much or as little as you wish. This technique takes a lot of thread and is time consuming...but well worth the effort.

Linen is the fabric used in this wrinkled example. It is crisp yet supple...the perfect fabric for this technique. It was wadded into a ball and tied, hence the random wrinkles with no distinct pattern.

This is a cotton fabric that was pleated in a vertical line. A double needle with a contrasting thread was used for the stitching on this wrinkled sample. If you wish the wrinkles to be the most prominant element on your piece, use matching thread.

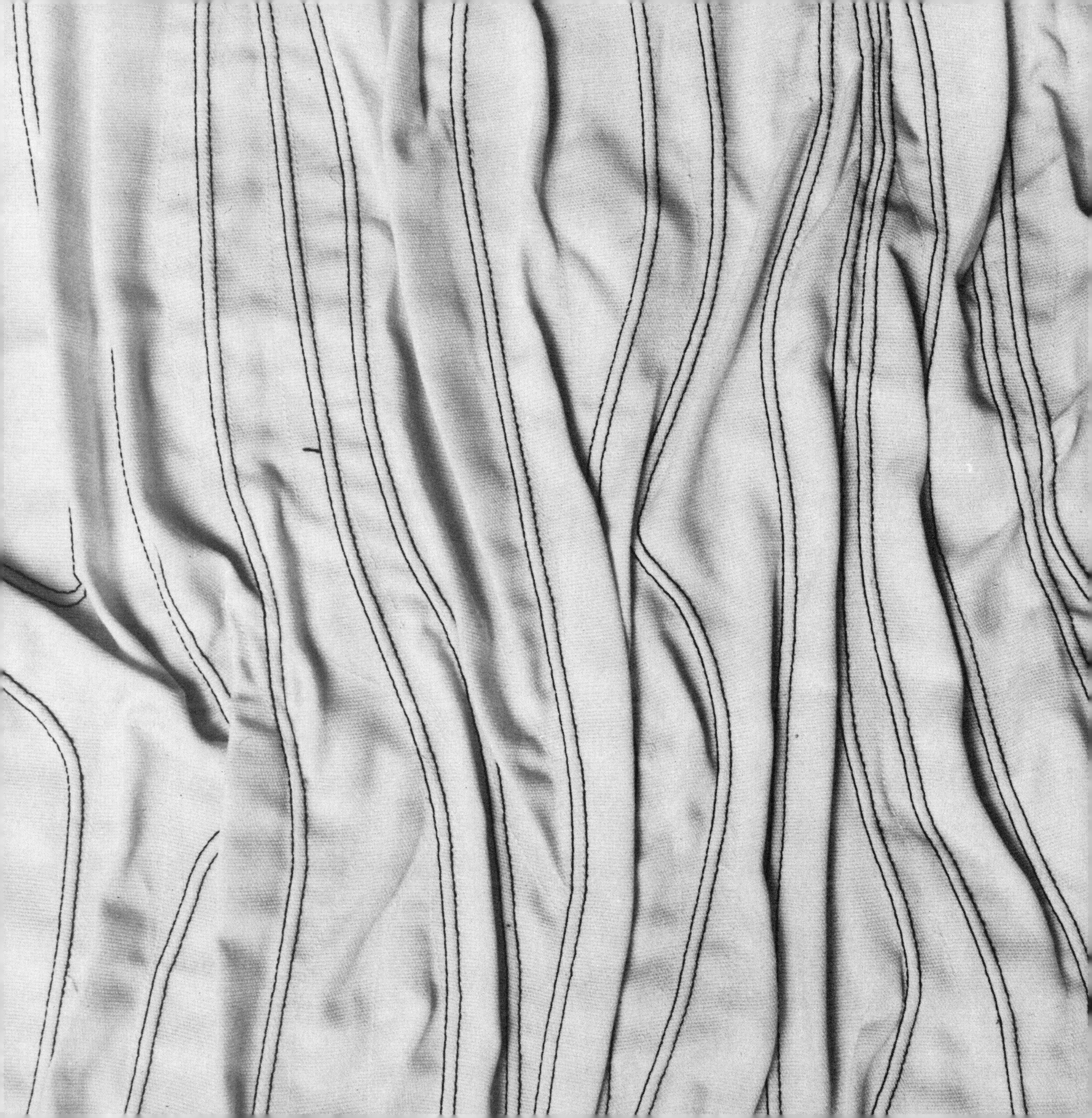

Raw silk is wrinkled/stitched on this sample. The larger wrinkles are wide enough to accommodate pieces of piping or other inserts that you might like to add. Simply place the piping under the large wrinkle and stitch it in place.

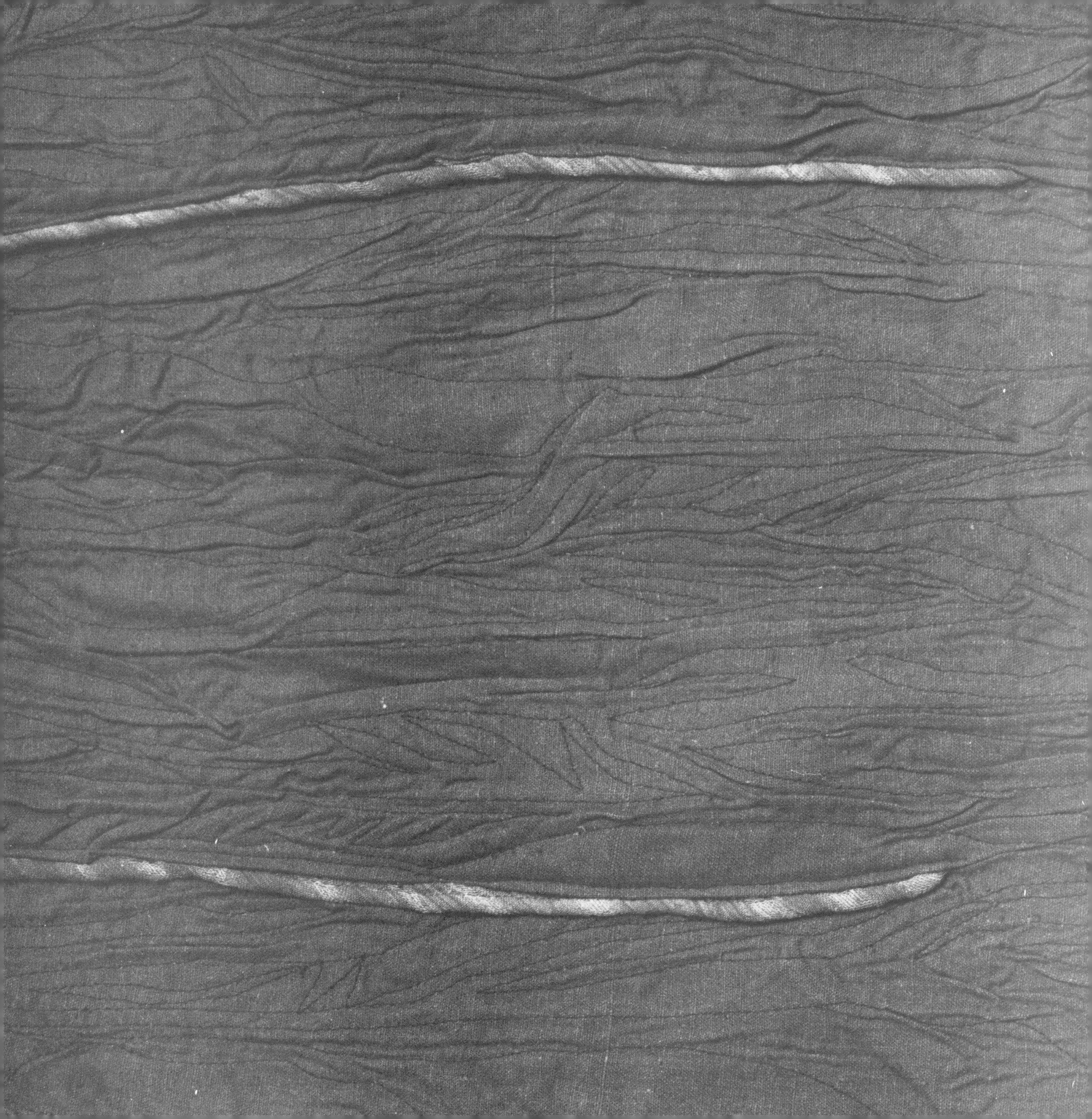

Wrinkling and stitching is not the only method to use to get a puckered or buckled effect. This piece by Ardyth Davis is a wonderful example of manipulating a fabric, in this case, muslin. The larger piece on the top is fastened to a smaller underlining piece... the excess has to go somewhere! So it gets pleated, folded, tied and stitched to make it fit. Notice the loose threads. Photo by Mollie Isaacs

Tucks & Pleats

Most of the tucks I've made and manipulated have been stripes because I like the movement that occurs with stripes, especially on garments. Another reason for choosing stripes is that there are lines to follow as you stitch the tucks.

It is easiest to do this technique if the width of the stripes you choose is 3 to 1 in ratio. If the stripes are even in size, especially 1/4" to 1/2" in width, the tucks are so close together that it is really time consuming.

I cut the fabric the length needed, and then start stitching the tucks, using the vertical stripes as my guide. When the piece is finished, I press the tucks from one end with all one color showing. Stitch across the tucks to keep them in that direction. I press the next section so the other color shows, then stitch. Continue until piece is all pressed and stitched.

The tucks are stitched straight across this striped cotton fabric.

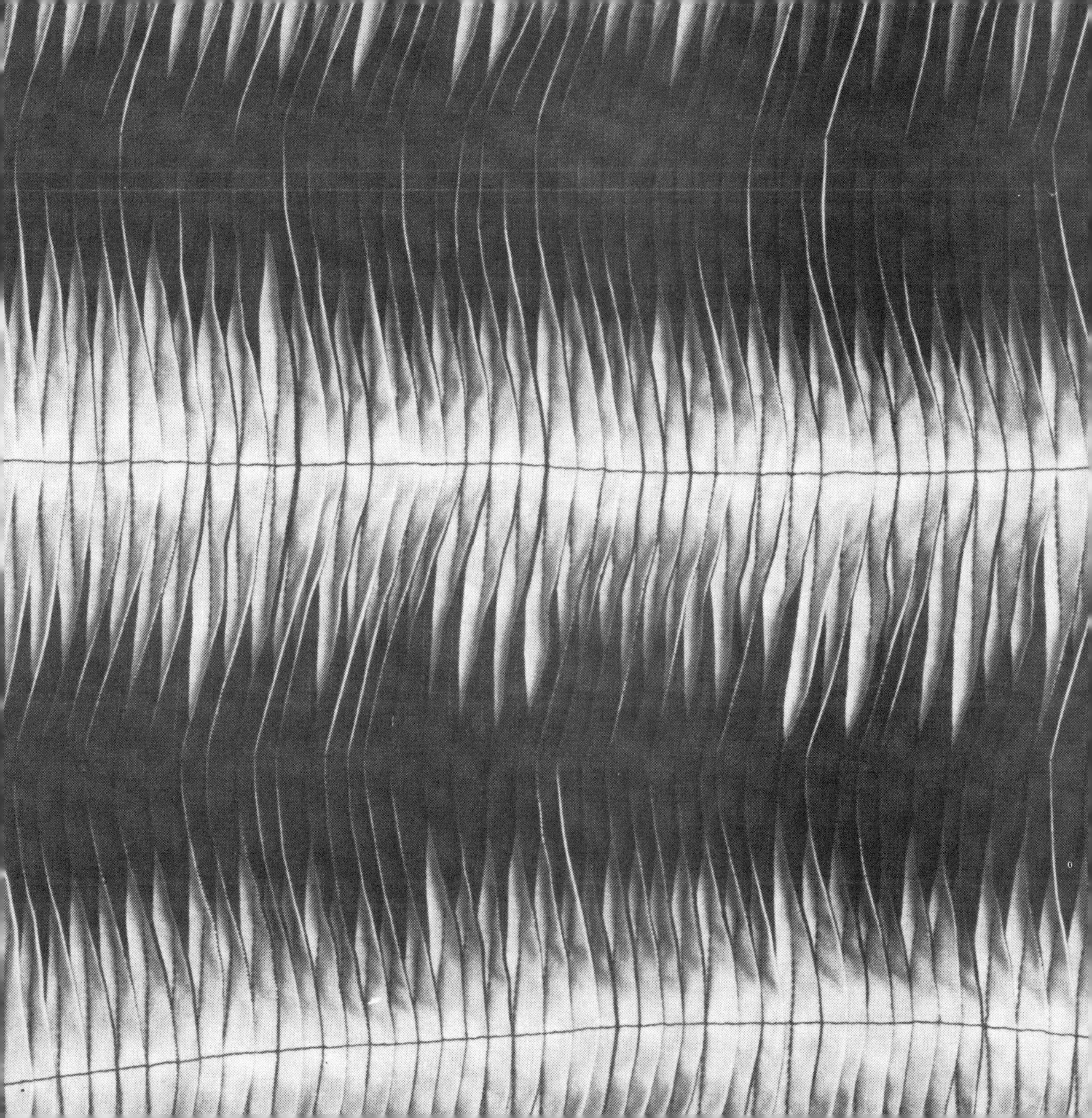

Curved lines are machine stitched on this piece to create an undulating effect.

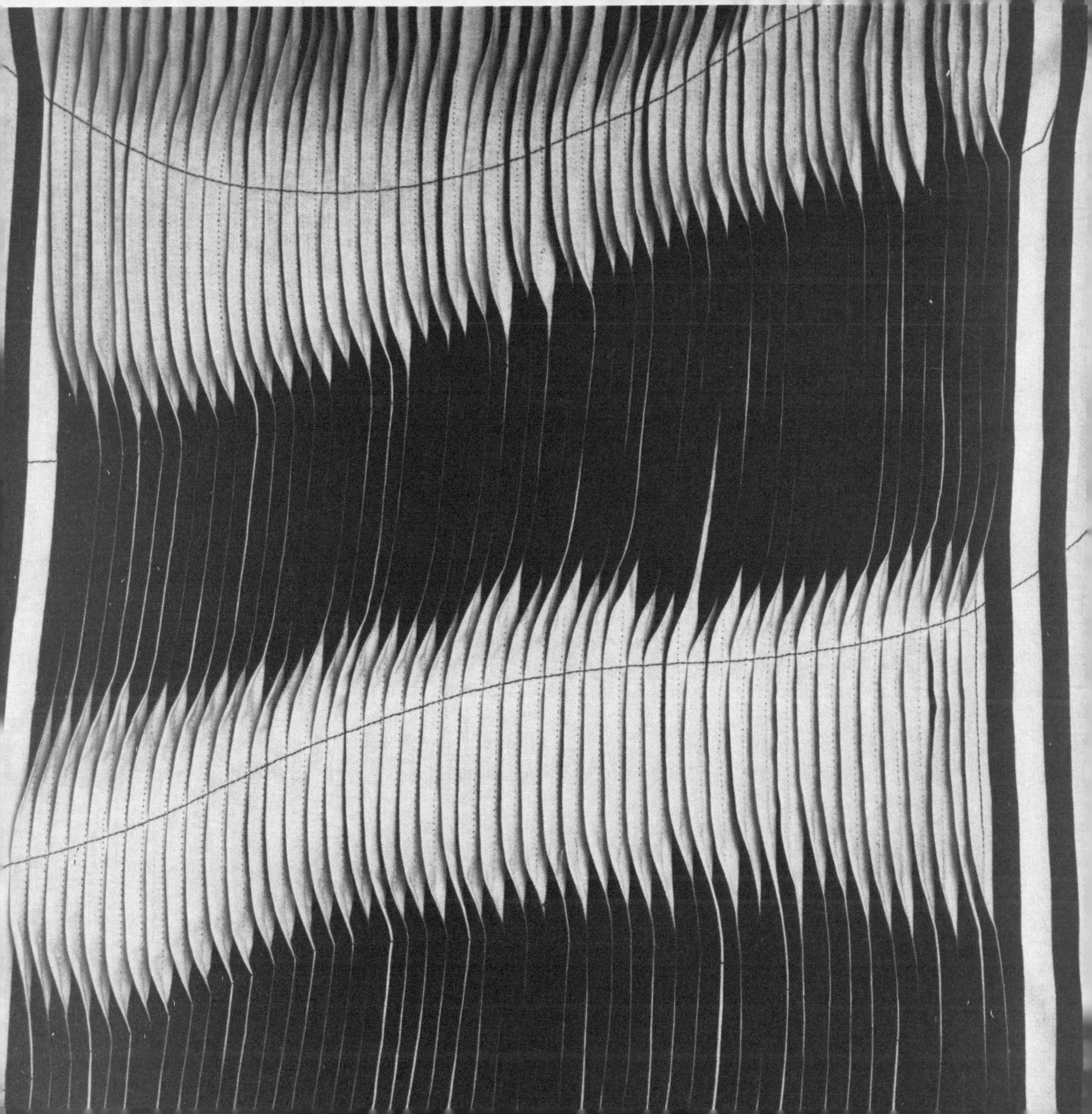

Diagonal lines are so dynamic, also flattering on a wearable piece. Possibly a stripe in a little more subtle combination might be a consideration if this were to be used in a garment.

This finely tucked commercial fabric has been re-tucked to give it more dimension. It was then pieced in various directions for an interesting effect.

This piece of soft silk has been pleated and tied.
The threads that hold the pleats together are fastened,
the ends left long for an additional design effect.
This piece and photo by Ardyth Davis.

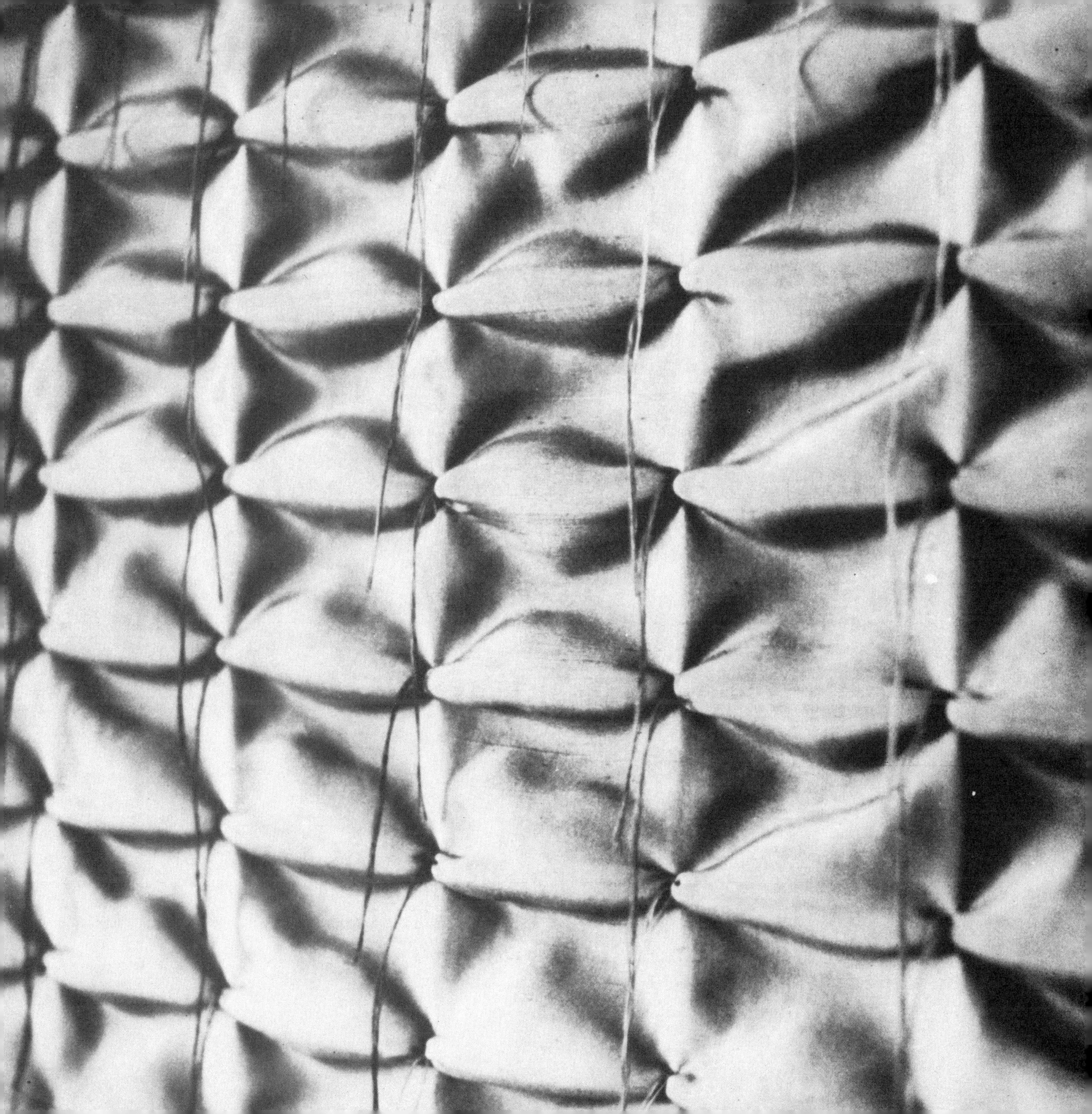

This sample is a combination of pleated and plain fabrics, same color. The pleats are pressed and each section is stitched at the ends to keep the pleats in place. Simple patchwork is used to put them together.

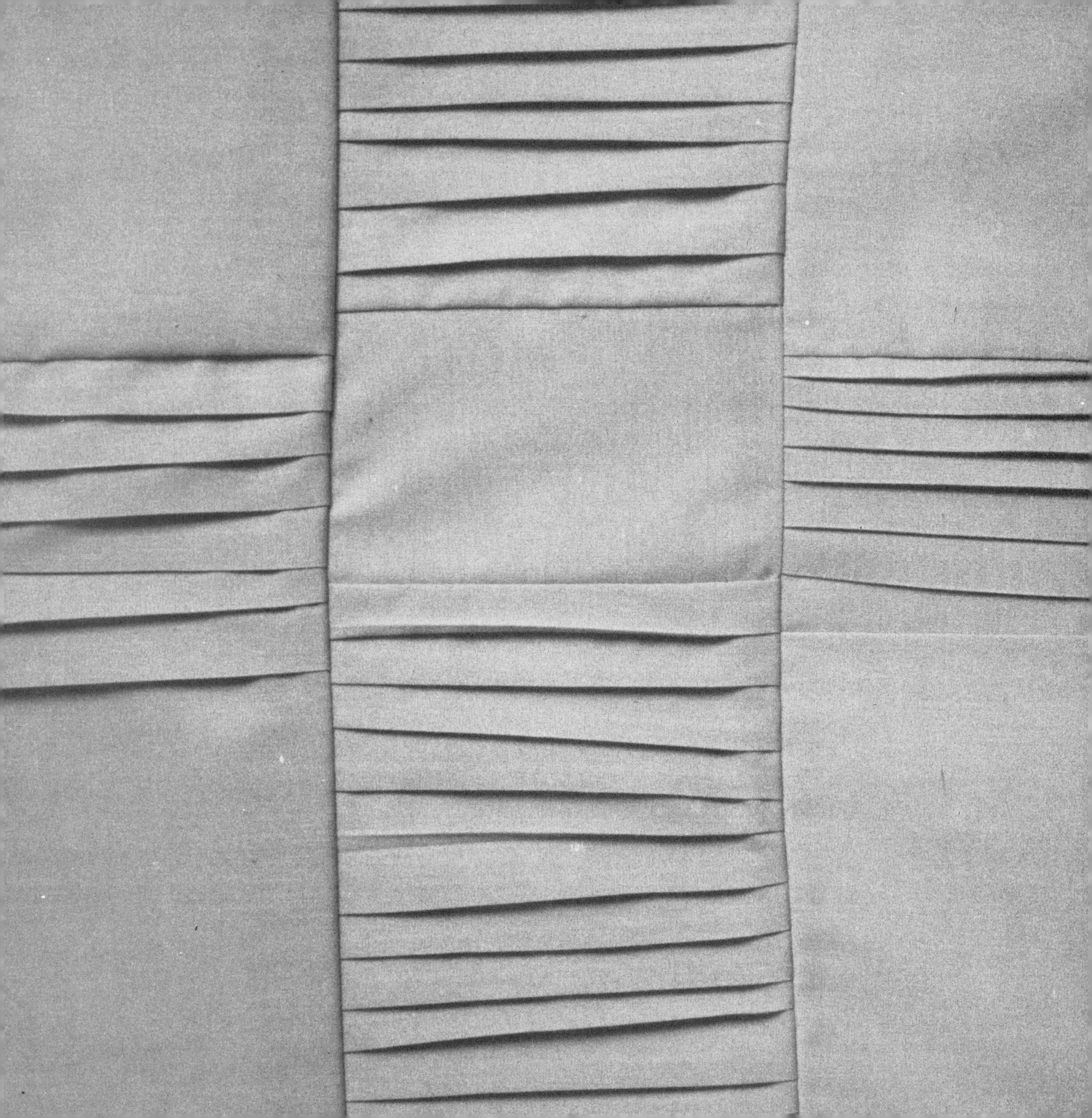

Pleats are combined with machine stitching...three different samples are shown. The first shows the 1" pleats with diagonal grid lines in two directions. The second shows the pleats with horizontal stitching to hold in place. The third shows just the pleats with stitching along the pressed edges.

A triangular shape was the beginning of this piece. The contrasting pieces on the sides were added and tucks were stitched. The original shape changed immediately and made the piece 'active'.

Trapunto

Trapunto is the method used to create an embossed surface. It is accomplished by machine or hand stitching a design and stuffing some of those spaces. These designated areas are usually stuffed from the back through a hole cut in the underlining or from an open end.

A layer of cotton fabric plus the underlining is the foundation of this sample. Machine stitching is added to define the shapes to be stuffed.

Draw a design on your fabric with your sewing or marking pens. Place the fabric on the underlining and stitch on your guidelines. Stuff as desired.

Tapered tucks are stitched, then stuffed. It is amazing how many techniques can be combined to set one's thinking on a new course...I've never stuffed a tuck before.

Pen & Ink

We are only going to touch on this technique that is related to fabric painting. It's fun to use permanent pens and India inks, which are also very permanent, as an alternative to fabric paint. Draw free-hand, use a ruler, re-emphasize lines on an existing print... dilute the India ink and use as a wash, try using a brayer (rubber roller) to spread it around..... NO LIMITS!

Simple lines, with a ruler and permanent pens, can be used to create pleasing designs.

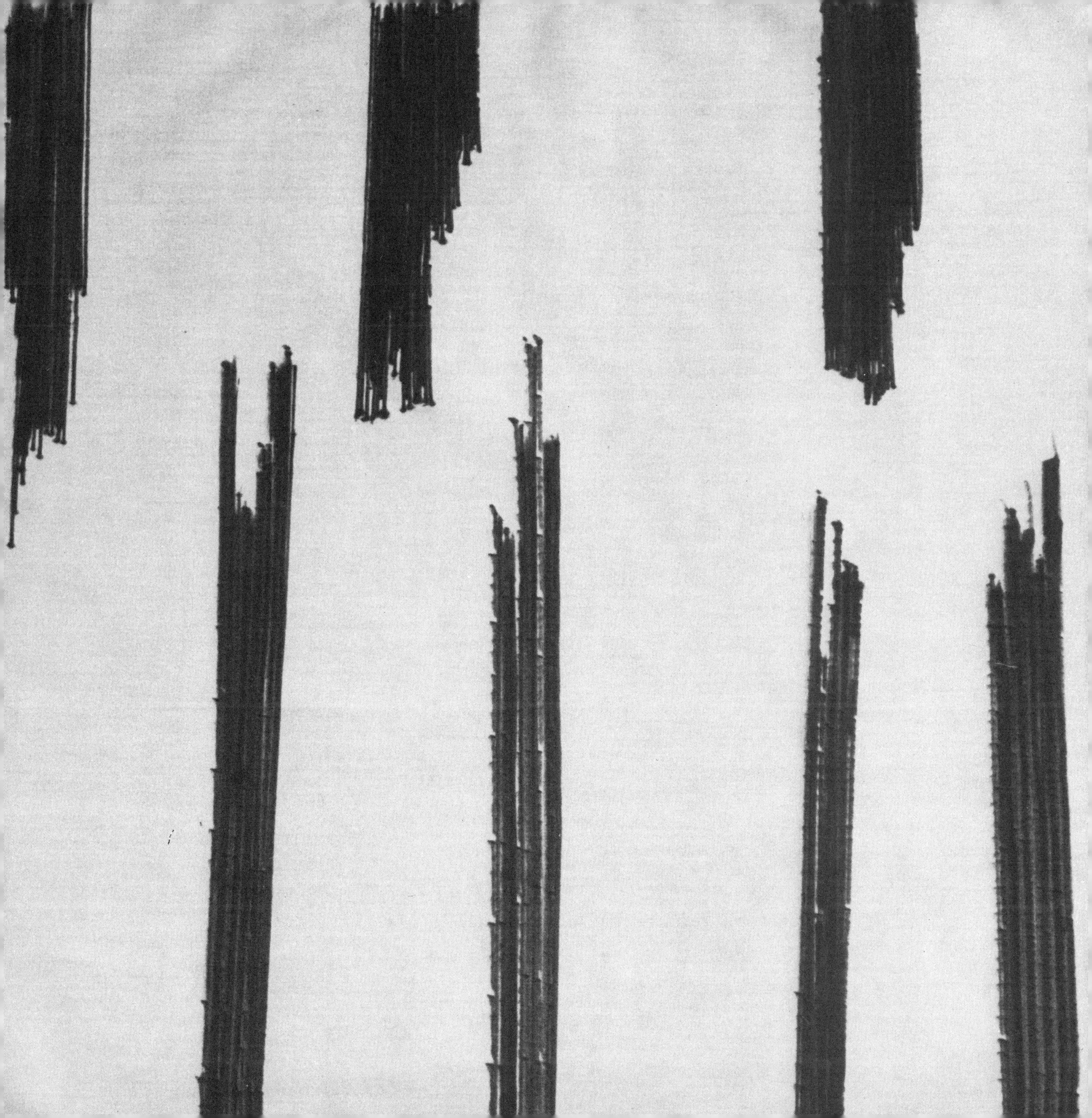

This piece, as the previous one, also uses a pen and ruler on the cotton fabric. It is slightly more intricate in design. See the next page for another possibility.

This is the same piece, as the previous page, just cut into strips and then pieced together...now the lines don't quite match...I like that.

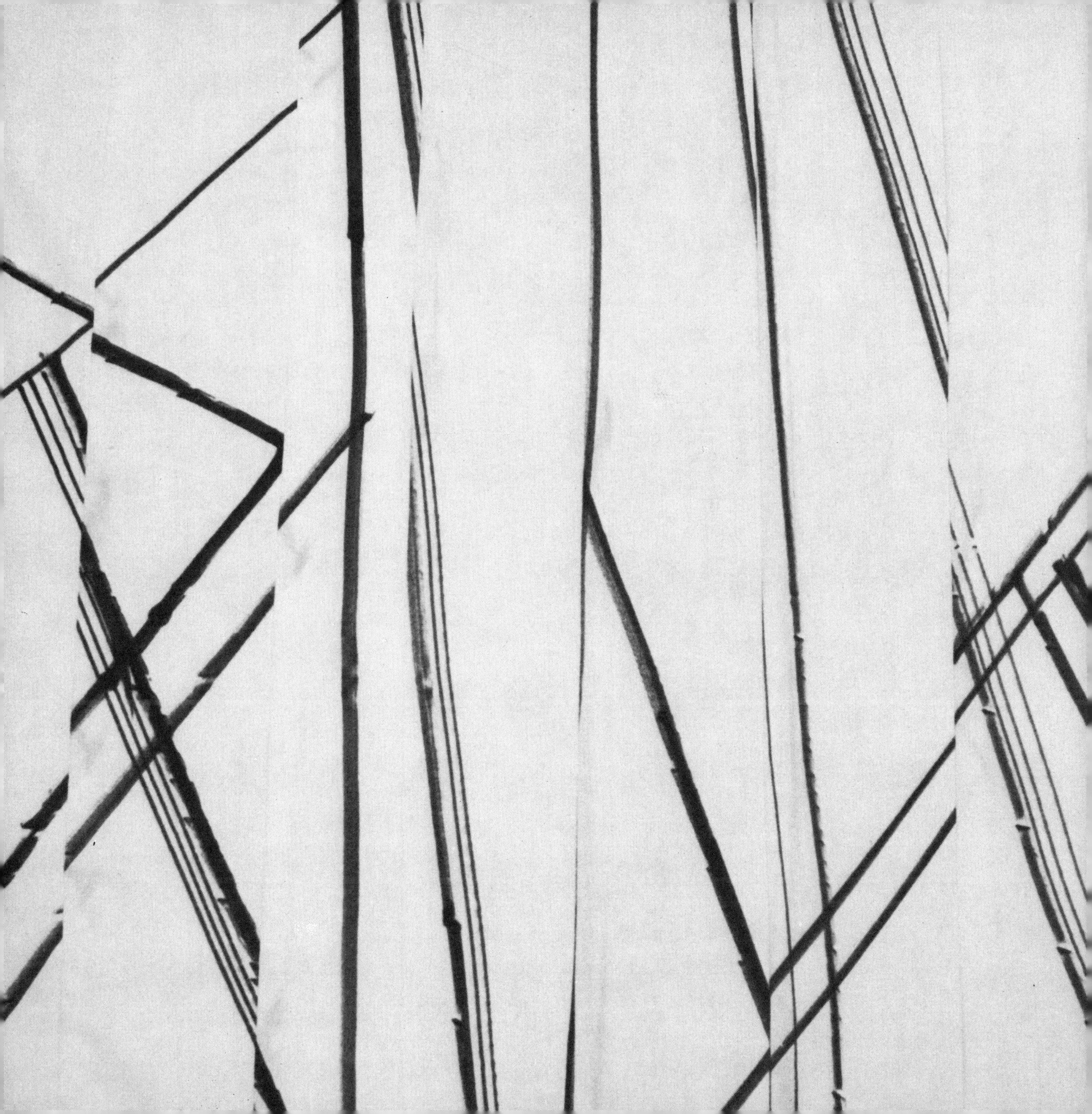

Diluted India ink is brushed on this cotton fabric, leaving an unpainted space near the middle. When it was dry I used the applicator to draw the lines on the sides. The beads were then sewn in place.

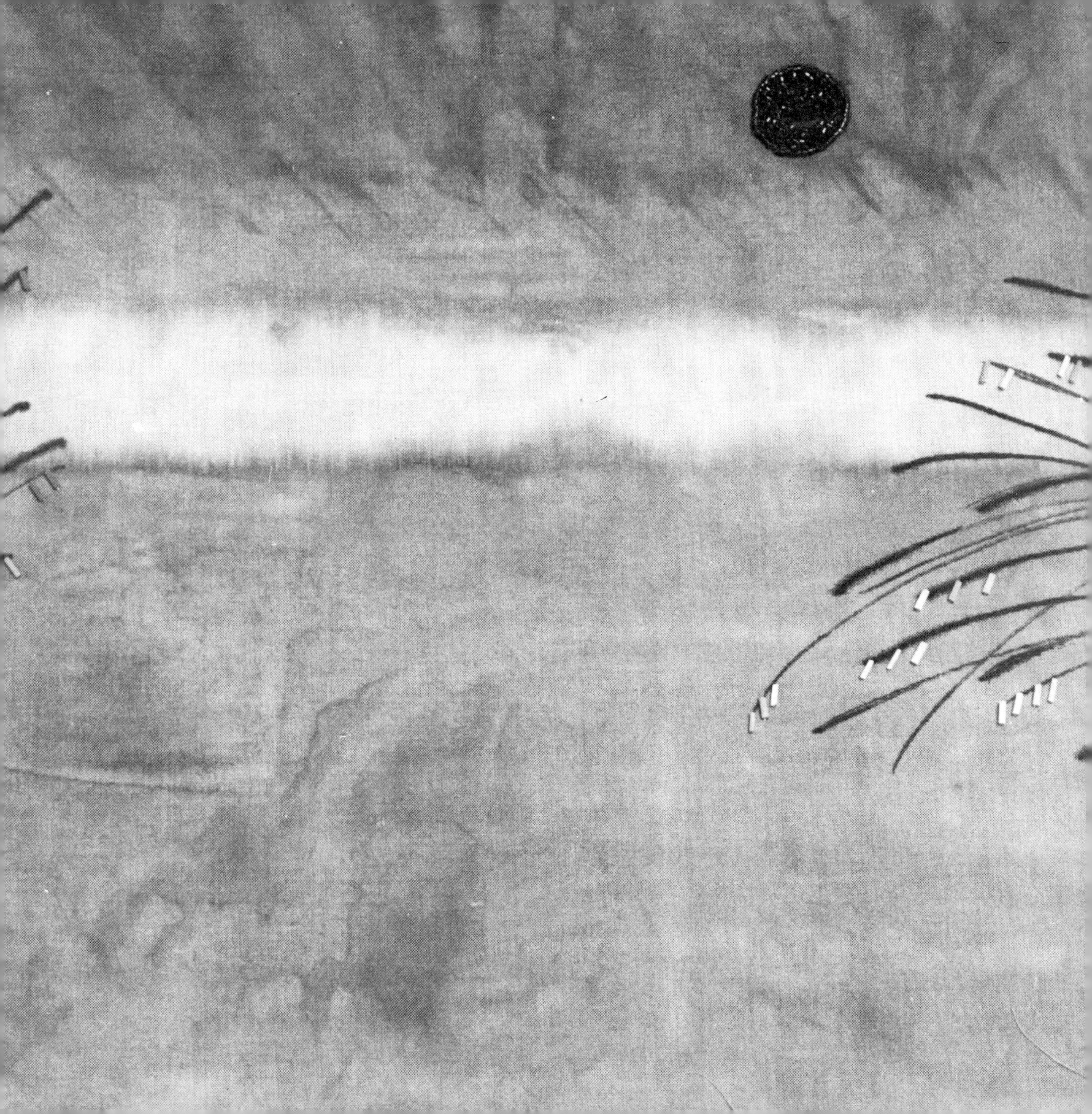

The base of this was also a wash with dark lines brushed on in a curvy pattern.

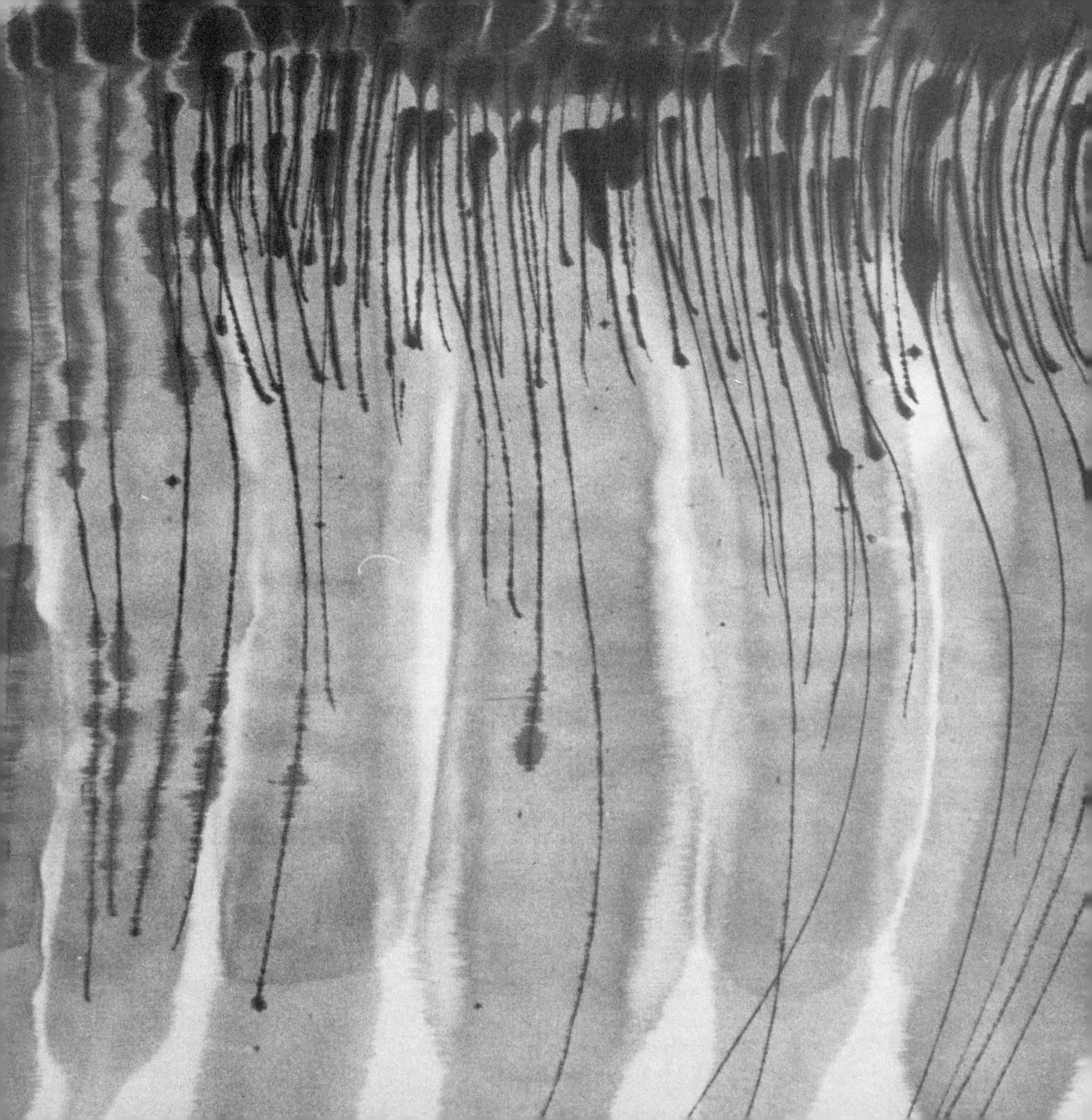

Lines were made with permanent pens on this cotton duck fabric. Curved sections were cut and each section was faced to finish the edge. The shapes were overlapped and stitched.

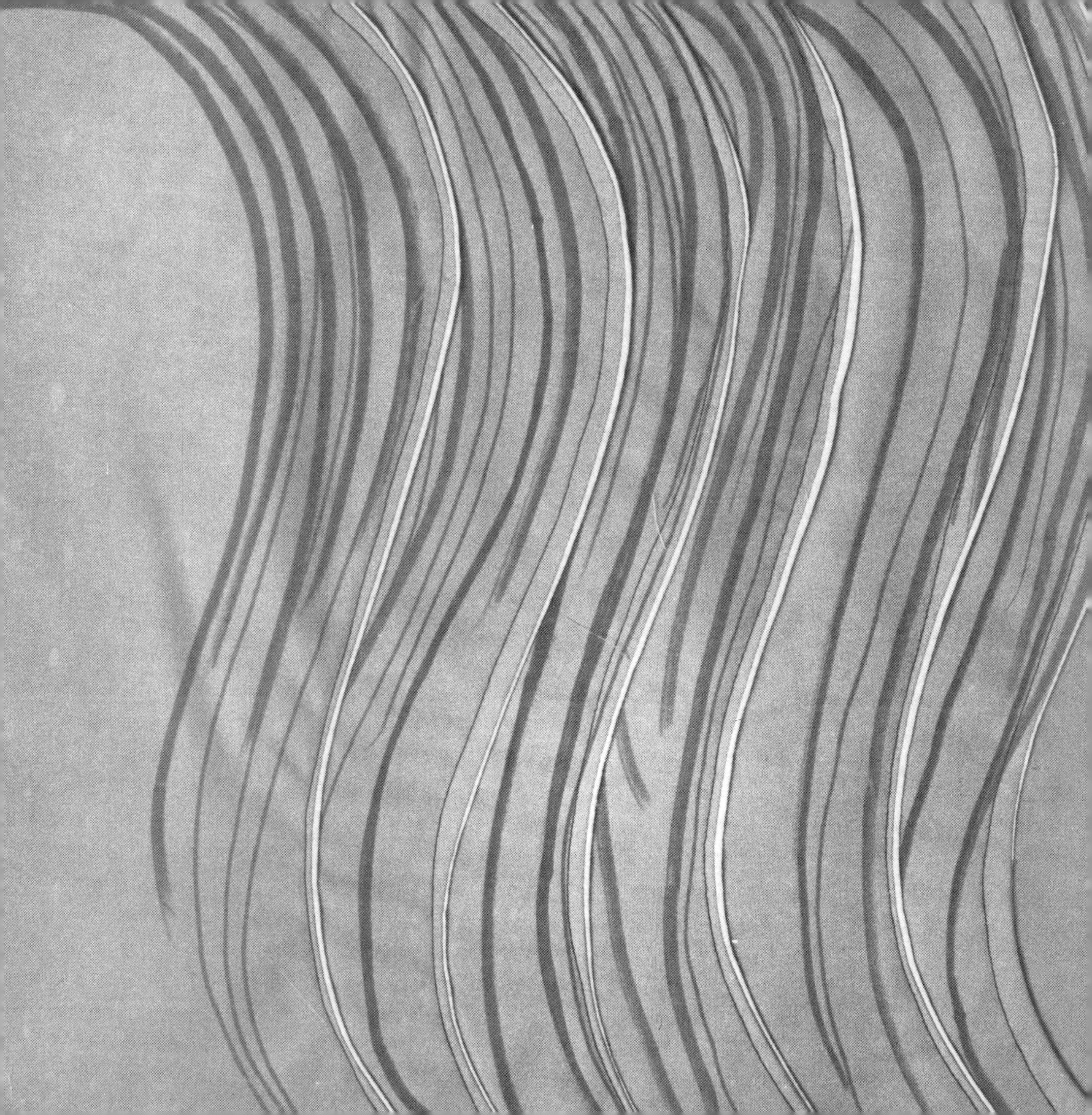

Sheer Overlays

Sheer fabrics can be used effectively in many of the techniques we have already explored. Using them just as an overlay can change the feeling and make-up of a piece instantly. The overlay diffuses the visual surface, protects the underlayer and can encompass small or hard to manage pieces.

This sheer overlay shows one corner folded back so the underlayer is more apparent. The underlayer consists of many pieces of sheer fabrics in various colors arranged on top of each other, for a shadowy effect. The organza on the top protects and covers this underlayer. Stitching through all the layers to repeat the shapes is the next step in this piece.

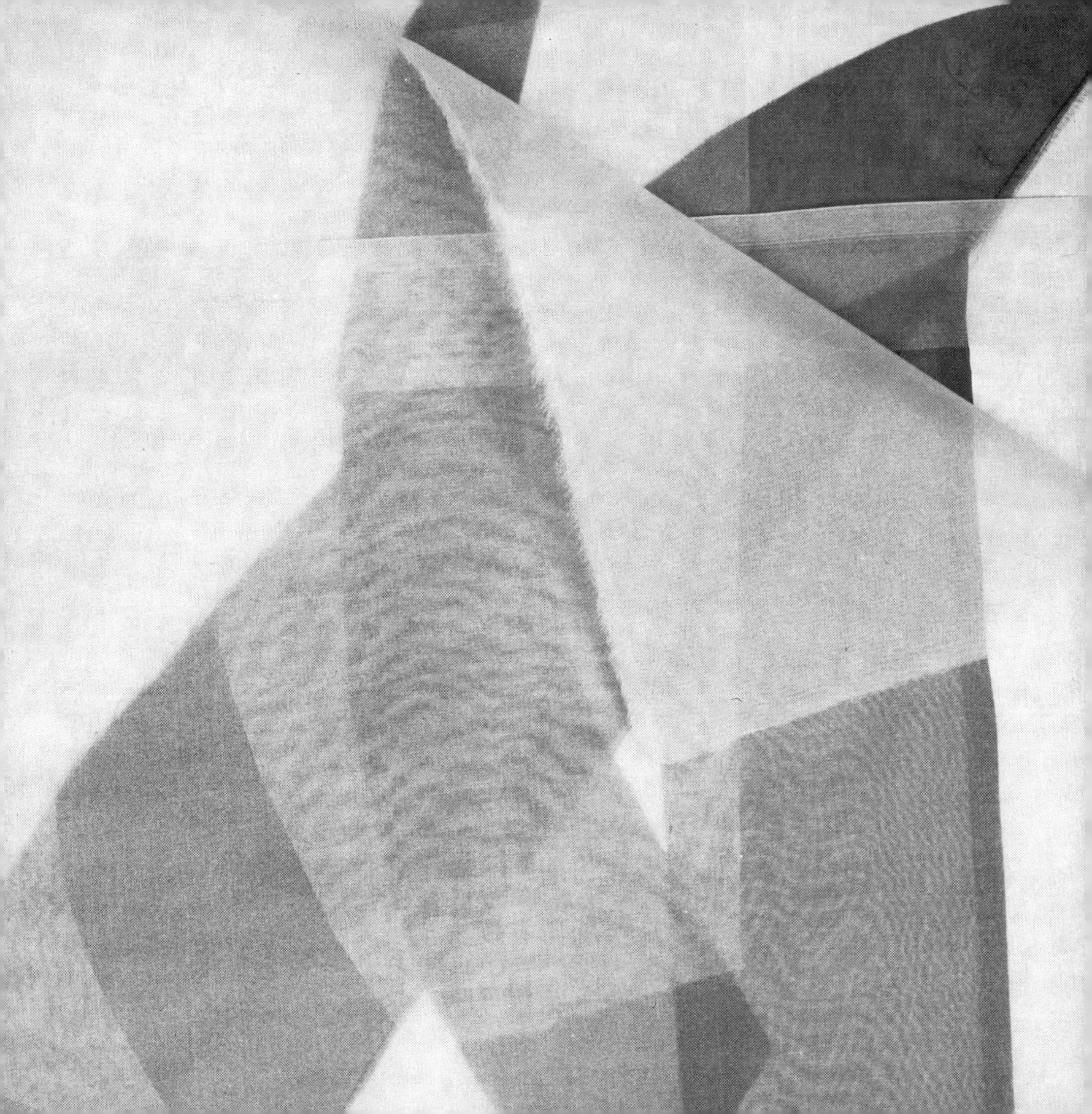

Heavy threads are tacked in a pattern and covered with the sheer fabric. These threads may move around somewhat....Some possibilities, maybe?

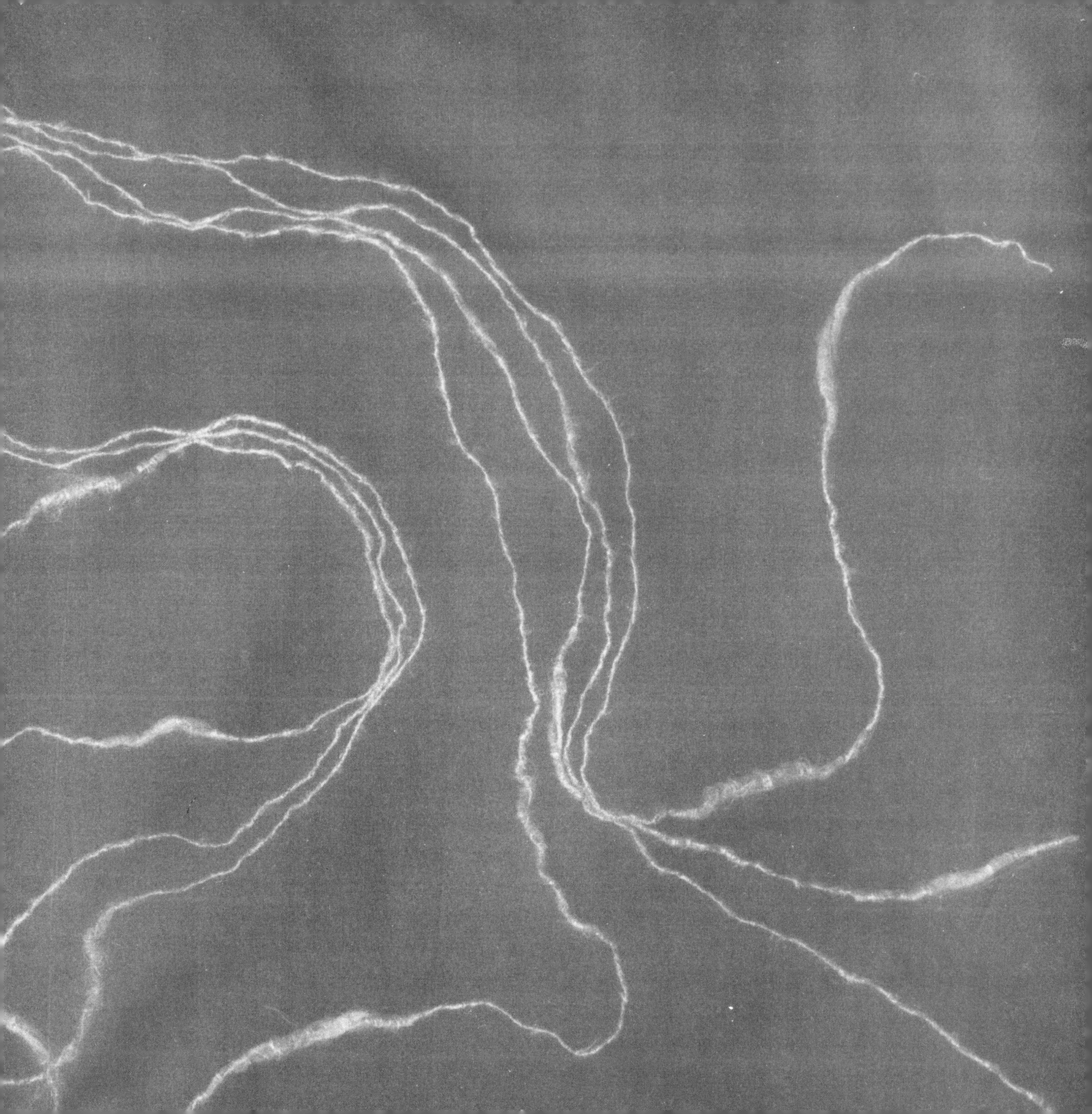

Lines were stitched on a sheer organza, then this fabric was placed over a striped linen. The sheer can be moved in such a way as to resemble a grid like graph paper or at any angle, as you see here.

This long rectangle of sheer fabric is folded, stitched at each side, turned and pressed. Textured yarn is placed in between the two layers and machine stitched. The stitching lines and the yarn are meant to resemble writing, as in a notebook. Notice the sewing thread left long at the ends of the lines.

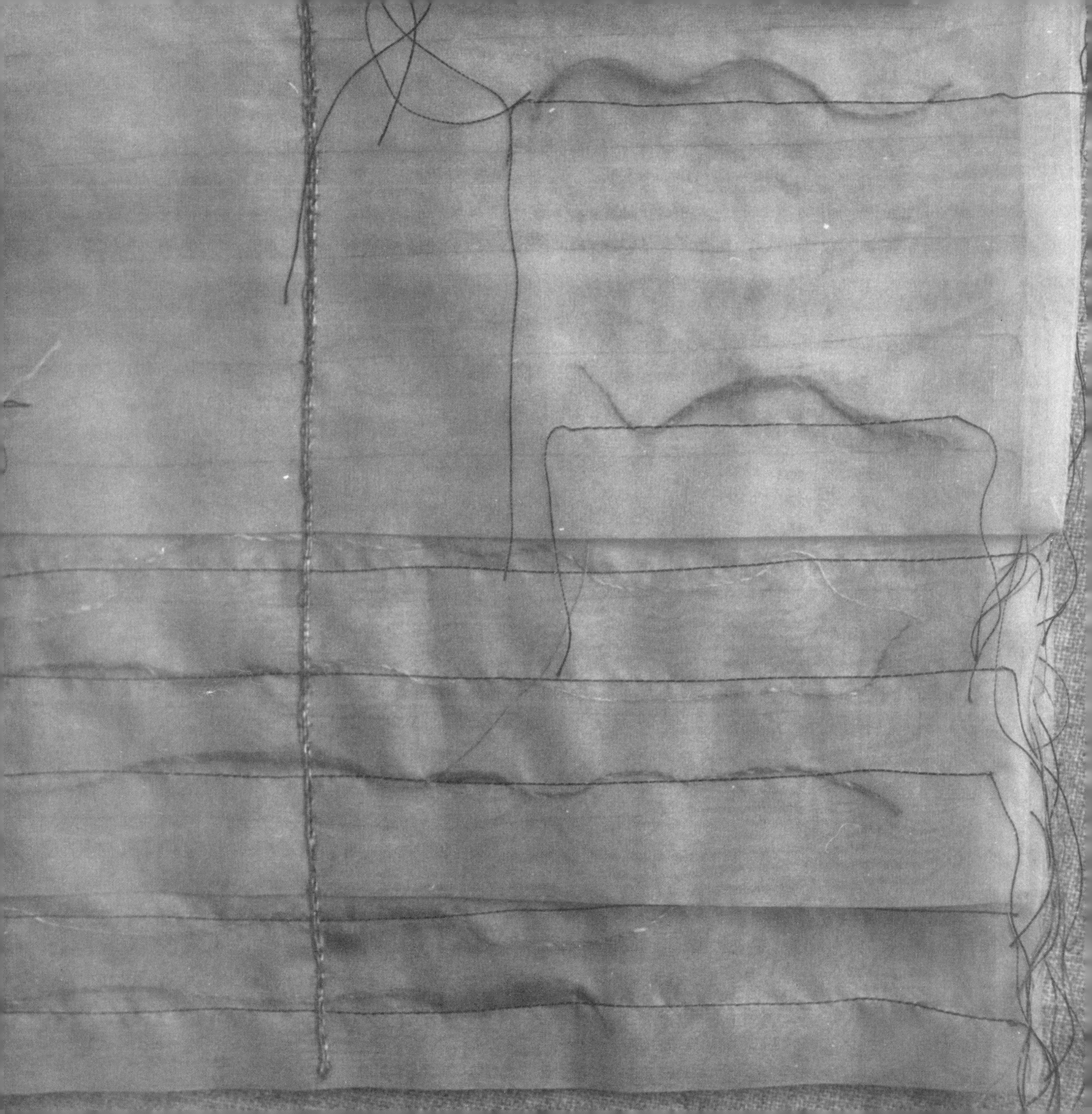

Miscellaneous

Squares of muslin have been folded in half diagonally. The two ends of the triangles are then folded to the center. The squares are overlapped and fastened.

In this example, canvas squares are cut from one corner diagonally to the center. Overlap the diagonal cuts to form a cup shape and glue to fasten. The shapes in the upper left corner are simply triangles, folded over and glued, then overlapped. This repetition of shape is so effective. Canvas is a great material to work with.... it's very firm, the edges need no finishing and it can be painted easily. This idea could easily be adapted to the concept of faced shapes.
These pieces and photos by Ardyth Davis.

Ravelled Edges

Start with a stack of 6 to 8 layers of cotton fabrics in various textures or colors. Stitch a pattern through all thicknesses and cut through to the layer you wish to display. Wash and dry in the machine for the maximum ravelling.

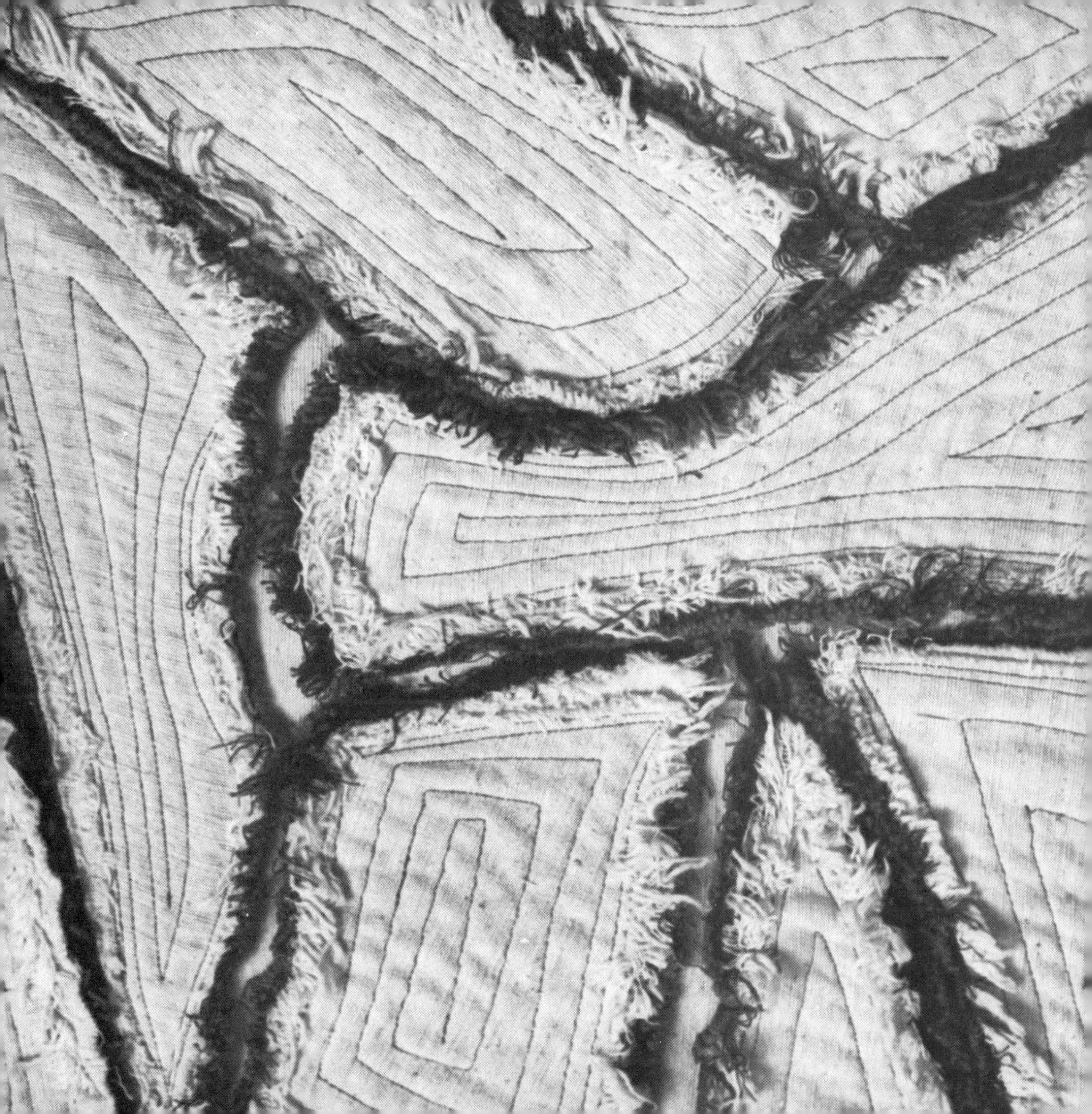

Serged Edges

Another tool that I use is an overlock machine to serge the edges of my fabric. These edges are usually utilitarian but can be decorative. Your zig-zag stitch on your sewing machine, very closely stitched, can also be used for a similar effect.

Burned Edges

To test a fabric to see if it is a natural or man-made fabric, I usually burn a little piece of it. If it is a natural fiber...it leaves an ash which smells like animals. If it is a man-made fiber, it usually melts. So, melting the cut edges was a fascinating idea to explore. Note: Use caution and work in a ventilated room.

Cotton Netting

Cotton mesh or netting was pulled on the bias and stitched to hold it in place. This mesh or one with bigger holes would make an unusual overlay or could be used to weave strips through.

Books

OTHER BOOKS BY LOIS ERICSON: Box 5222, Salem, OR 97304

"Pleats" $15
Contemporary use of pleated fabric
80 pgs., 16 in color

"Texture...A Closer Look" $22
224 pgs. 200 photos. 16 pgs of color.
Manipulate, create textured surfaces
from ordinary material

"Design & Sew It Yourself" $15
A workbook for creative clothing

"Belts...Waisted Sculpture" $12
An idea book of more than 50 belts

"Print It Yourself" $7
Fabric painting

Postage and Handling $2.50 for 1-4 books, U.S. Funds

William Faulkner once said--

"You can't eat for 8 hours a day,
nor drink for 8 hours a day,
nor make love for 8 hours a day.
All you can do for 8 hours is <u>work</u>."

Bibliography

Brodatz, Phil. Textures. N.Y.: Dover Publ., 1966.

Feininger, Andreas. Nature Close Up. N.Y.: Dover Publ., 1977.

________________. Stone and Man. N.Y.: Dover Publ., 1961.

Franck, Frederick. Art as a Way. N.Y.: Crossroad Publ., 1981.

________________. The Zen of Seeing. N.Y.: Vintage Books Random House, 1973.

Komanecky, M. and Butera, V. The Folding Image. New Haven, Ct.: Yale Univ. Art Gallery, 1984.

Kubota, Itchiku. Opulence. Tokyo Kodansha Int'l Ltd., 1984.

Llewellyn, J.J. The World of the Dark Crystal. N.Y.: A. Knopf Publ., 1982.

Marnat, Marcel. Klee. N.Y.: Leon Ameil Publ., 1974.

Mathiessen, Peter. The Tree Where Man Was Born. N.Y.: E.P. Dutton & Co., 1972.

Oka, Hideyuki. How To Wrap 5 More Eggs. N.Y. & Tokyo: Weatherhill, 1980.

Proctor, Richard. The Principles of Pattern. N.Y.: Van Nostrand Renhold, 1969.

Reich, Hanns. The World From Above. N.Y.: Hill & Wang, 1966.

Robinson, David. Reflections. N.Y.: Holt, Reinhart & Winston, 1978.

Rudofsky, Bernard. Architecture Without Architects. N.Y.: Doubleday & Co., 1964.

Samuels, Mike & Nancy. Seeing With The Mind's Eye. Random House (N.Y.) and Bookworks Book (Berkeley), 1975.

Sutton, Ann & Myron. The Wild Places. N.Y.: Harper & Row, 1972.

Tokugawa Art Museum. The Shogun Age Exhibition. Toppan Printing Co. Ltd., 1983.

White, Jan. Graphic Idea Notebook. N.Y.: Watson-Guptill Publ., 1980.

Wichmann, Siegfried. Japonisme. N.Y.: Harmony Books, 1980.

Periodicals: National Geographic
GEO
American Craft
FMR

Guest Artist

Ardyth Davis, my guest artist, has an impressive art resumé and background. Her work is in numerous commercial buildings in the Washington, D.C. area, and she has been invited to show in some prestigious exhibitions. In addition to all her admirable talents and traits... she has a wonderful sense of humor, an asset and a necessity.

She makes her home in Leesburg, Va. with her husband, two sons, and various pets. She lives in the country, as I do, so we share our love of nature as well as our art interests.

Ardyth Davis
Rt. 2 Box 99F
Leesburg, Va. 22075

Author

Photo by Jean Hudson

My physical world centers around my home in the high Sierras.

My personal milieu revolves around my husband, Lennart, and my family.

My work focus for the past four years has been on designing and making limited editions and one-of-a-kind clothes. Presenting seminars and workshops all over the country is very special to me ...a time to connect with other artists and sewing enthusiasts.

Since I have become more involved with texture and fabric manipulation...I seem to have come full circle - to constructed wall pieces again. I find it fascinating to have so many choices in one art medium.

Lois Ericson
Box 5222
Salem, OR 97304